M000118122

# PRAISE FOR #KeepGoing

Mari Tautimes' painfully honest account of her very challenging life—laid bare—is an emotional, inspiring tour de force. It reminded me that all of us are struggling and need help from time to time, and that we're all capable of far more than we may believe. Full of tragedy, self-discovery, and remarkable perseverance, this lovely book is the living embodiment of Winston Churchill's famous line, "If you're going through hell, keep going."

**—Mike Paton**
*Certified EOS Implementer®, coauthor of Get a Grip*


Mari is someone who has seemingly faced all the odds but continues to have the tenacity to stay in the game anyway. While most people will be satisfied with "insights" and "awareness" in their personal development, Mari's dedication to take action, implement what she learns, and push through uncomfortable moments are what continue to produce tangible results. It's been such an incredible gift to watch Mari's journey from grit to grace.

**—Shasheen Shah**
*CEO of Coherent Strategies Consulting and Coaching, author of The Kid and the King*

I had the pleasure of having Mari Tautimes join my Siriusly Authentic Squad. Mari's passion, tenacity, and authenticity were a great inspiration for all in my squad. Mari is an excellent storyteller who delivers powerful nuggets that will resonate with the masses.

—**Siri Lindley**
*World champion triathlete, performance and life coach, author of Surfacing: From the Depths of Self-Doubt to Winning Big and Living Fearlessly*


Mari Tautimes' drive to survive, and then ultimately to thrive, brilliantly shines through in *#KeepGoing*.

This book chronicles Mari's journey from a teenage unwed mother to a lifelong learner, successful entrepreneur, wife, and mother. Her journey is not for the faint of heart but is a read that draws you in with its authenticity, vulnerability, and dedication to giving the reader a glimpse into what it takes to power through when life seems stacked against you.

I recommend this book for anyone that needs a reminder that life can be hard, but with focus, commitment, and a willingness to learn and grow, you can build a beautiful life from wherever you start if you *#KeepGoing*.

—**Margie Taylor**
*Co-Founder and CEO of Audacious Studios*

# #KeepGoing

## FROM 15-YEAR-OLD MOM TO
## SUCCESSFUL CEO & ENTREPRENEUR

# Mari Tautimes

# #KeepGoing

## FROM 15-YEAR-OLD MOM TO
## SUCCESSFUL CEO & ENTREPRENEUR

## Mari Tautimes

Advantage.

Copyright © 2021 by Mari Tautimes.

All rights reserved. No part of this book may be used or reproduced in any manner whatsoever without prior written consent of the author, except as provided by the United States of America copyright law.

Published by Advantage, Charleston, South Carolina.
Member of Advantage Media Group.

ADVANTAGE is a registered trademark, and the Advantage colophon is a trademark of Advantage Media Group, Inc.

Printed in the United States of America.

10  9  8  7  6  5  4  3  2  1

ISBN: 978-1-64225-344-3
LCCN: 2021915990

Cover design by David Taylor.
Layout design by Analisa Smith.

This publication is designed to provide accurate and authoritative information in regard to the subject matter covered. It is sold with the understanding that the publisher is not engaged in rendering legal, accounting, or other professional services. If legal advice or other expert assistance is required, the services of a competent professional person should be sought.

Advantage Media Group is proud to be a part of the Tree Neutral® program. Tree Neutral offsets the number of trees consumed in the production and printing of this book by taking proactive steps such as planting trees in direct proportion to the number of trees used to print books. To learn more about Tree Neutral, please visit **www.treeneutral.com**.

Advantage Media Group is a publisher of business, self-improvement, and professional development books and online learning. We help entrepreneurs, business leaders, and professionals share their Stories, Passion, and Knowledge to help others Learn & Grow. Do you have a manuscript or book idea that you would like us to consider for publishing? Please visit **advantagefamily.com**.

*To Andrew*

# CONTENTS

Foreword . . . . . . . . . . . . . . . . . . . . . . . . . . . . . . . . . . xiii

Preface . . . . . . . . . . . . . . . . . . . . . . . . . . . . . . . . . . . xvii

Introduction . . . . . . . . . . . . . . . . . . . . . . . . . . . . . . . . 1

How to Use This Book . . . . . . . . . . . . . . . . . . . . . . . . . 3

PART 1:
**My Story: From Teen Mom to CEO** . . . . . . . . . . . . . . 5

1.1
**"I'll Just Punch You in the Stomach..."** . . . . . . . . . . . . 7

1.2
**In an Instant, My Brother Was Gone** . . . . . . . . . . . . 21

1.3
**Time Bombs** . . . . . . . . . . . . . . . . . . . . . . . . . . . . . . . 27

1.4
**Living on Purpose** . . . . . . . . . . . . . . . . . . . . . . . . . . 71

PART 2:
**Designing Your Life** . . . . . . . . . . . . . . . . . . . . . . . . . 97

2.1
**Are You Ready to Create Your Dream Life?** . . . . . . 103

# FOREWORD

Life is hard, but harder for some people than others. As a student of history who is deeply curious about contemporary human motivation and grit, I am fascinated by stories of courageous individuals who, for whatever reason, are able to take control of their circumstances and persevere, survive, and then thrive. This is one of those stories.

When I met Mari Tautimes in 2014, she was working at a local insurance company, looking to expand the family business. She was the consummate professional who was always prepared and ready to help. As we got to know each other better, she started to share her background and some of her personal stories. It became clear that in addition to being a good businesswoman, she had overcome tremendous adversity in almost every aspect of her life—a young woman raising a child out of wedlock, a difficult family life, trying to earn a living and make her way in the world. Trying to find a way to survive and manage her circumstances without a clear road map, role model, or economic advantage. The more we talked, the more I learned, and the more impressed I became. This was an extraordinary story of overcoming the odds, an inspiring story of accomplishment, perseverance, and belief.

As we started to work together on some projects, it became clear that Mari was not only driven by her personal goals; she was supremely motivated to help others in all aspects of her life. Mari has many great attributes: (1) She has overcome tremendous obstacles in her life. (2) She is a lifelong learner and has natural curiosity about nearly everything. (3) She has a big heart and takes personal responsibility for all her endeavors. (4) She wants to make a difference for herself, her family, and the world. (5) She now has a track record of extraordinary achievements accomplished by first figuring it out for herself and then helping others along the way. And, as I sometimes remind her, she is just getting started.

In fact, when I asked Mari why she wrote this book, her answer was a clear explanation of intention and an indication of who she is as a person. "I want to help and inspire people, and I think that if someone reads this story and realizes that it is possible to change their future, it will be worth it. If I had read a book like this, it might have made a difference." This statement is completely unassuming, open hearted, and accurate. It's a great reason to share your personal stories of tragedy and heartbreak, hardships and abuse, impossible challenges and curveballs.

Mari's personal story is compelling enough, but then she adds more value by outlining her 7 Simple Steps (not easy steps, but simple) to take account of where you are and begin the challenging process of substantial change. Lots of people want to do better but many need either a reminder or instructions set to put the plan in motion. This book can act as a blueprint for taking control of your life, understanding what is important, shedding the insignificant, and focusing on goals that are important to you—all rolled into 150 pages.

We see it all the time in popular culture: the movie version (even the TikTok version) makes it seem so simple and easy. Individuals who will themselves to success. They magically find a way to rise to the top and get what they want. They leverage their superpower to win. The reason this type of story is so compelling is because it rarely happens in real life. It rarely happens in real life because it's incredibly hard, requires years of mental, emotional, and physical work internally and externally, and most people aren't up for the journey. But it is possible, and this book is an outline of one way to do it. So if you are not comfortable with where you are in life, if you think you can do better, if you are open to suggestions and willing to do the hard work, read this book.

When I first met Mari, I told her: "You are Mari Tautimes. You can do anything"—which I say to just about everyone I meet. It's a bit of a personal trademark for me to remind everyone I connect with that in a world of blaming, canceling, and constant negativity, if you create an intention and a plan and have the commitment and perseverance to keep going regardless of the odds, most anyone can figure it out. There is no magic. Rarely is there a superpower involved. My experience is if something is so important to you that you are willing to sacrifice and prioritize to achieve it—then you have a good shot of making it happen. Just like this book.

Writing a book is hard, especially one that is about your personal story. This is a great read because it's interesting, thoughtful, helpful, and inspiring. Plus, I know how it ends (or at least the update in 2021), and it might be the key to your future.

—**Dan Tyre**, sales director of HubSpot, serial entrepreneur, and author of *Inbound Organization: How to Build and Strengthen Your Company's Future Using Inbound Principles*

# PREFACE

There are so many points in my life when I can remember feeling defeated and almost certain that maybe emotional and financial peace were things that were only accessible to other people, or maybe even not at all.

I would think that maybe life is just hard now, and it always will be, and the only real pure moments of peace and joy are the moments we experienced as innocent children.

After that, once our consciousness is awakened, we just have to do our best to get through, and what we're really working toward is being qualified to make it into whatever one's version of the afterlife is.

In these moments of defeat and reflection, my very next thought is, *no freaking way*. Except I use the actual f-word, but I don't want to scare you off in the first four paragraphs of my book.

What I have decided to believe instead is that life doesn't have to be hard. Sure, it will have hard moments, but that's different than having a hard life.

I have been on an obsessive mission to find or create a treasure map where the X represents a final destination where:

- My past does not equal my future.

- I know how to set boundaries and stand up for myself.

- My relationships are mutually beneficial and reciprocated.

- I know how to keep my head trash in check.

- I have achieved financial peace.

- My time is spent more on the art of fulfillment vs. the science of achievement.

As I worked through my life at home, I was also trying to leverage our entrepreneurial family business as a way for us to get up and out. But it seemed that the same forces of hardship applied there too.

In our business, I felt like we had to give up our lives for the cause. We never felt like we were in control, we were eking out profitability, but not at the rate we felt we should be. Our processes were nonexistent, and we weren't clear on our priorities at any given time, so we did everything, all the time, based on feeling and emotion rather than information and data.

In both cases, though, I saw other people that weren't having that same experience. People that were leading really great lives and running really great businesses.

I wanted that for *my* life. For *our* business. And I was on a mission to get it and was certain that I could because it didn't make sense to me that some people get to "have it all" and so many others do not. In my mind, there was plenty to go around, and I wanted to get mine. I wanted our family to get ours.

My mission to figure it out really started in 2013. I was thirty-three, I had four kids, I was weighing in at 260 pounds, I managed fifteen employees, and I discovered it was time for massive changes and shifts in my life because I felt like I wasn't getting *anywhere*.

The bald wheels of my life were spinning in mud and splattering it all back in my face on a daily basis.

I also discovered that if something was going to change, it was going to have to be me. I needed to get new information, new ideas, and new methods to make a shift in my life. I was tired of the struggle.

I'm very lucky that I made it out. But I couldn't really see beyond the "getting out." I knew I wanted to help as many other people as I could that found themselves in the same position, but I wasn't sure exactly how to do it.

For the entrepreneurial side, I became an EOS Implementer®, which means I get to help entrepreneurial companies just like mine figure out how to get control, increase profitability, and get everything they want out of their businesses through EOS®, or the Entrepreneurial Operating System.

For the life side, I am sharing my story in the hope that it is helpful and inspiring to anyone that needs to see what's possible and how I navigated my journey. I also share a tools and insights segment through a simple seven-step process that I've pulled together from my own analysis of important things I've learned from Tony Robbins, Stephen Covey, Brené Brown, Keith Cunningham, and EOS that I've used over the years to create a plan and execute that plan.

My hope is that I can be a conduit or pathway to all of the amazing teachers, books, podcasts, and systems that I have had the opportunity to learn from and that with this work, people can start to take steps toward creating the life that they deserve.

# INTRODUCTION

Congratulations and welcome! If you've picked up this book, it's likely because you are seeking inspiration, motivation, and/or nuggets you can use for your own life and career and/or entrepreneurial journey.

In it, I pull together my insights from twenty-plus years in business, thousands of hours of coaching and training, and concepts from as many books and podcasts as I could squeeze in while raising a family, digging deep to discover myself and to eventually push back until I was able to get the life that I felt I deserved.

To be clear, I don't have all the answers. In fact, the more answers I discover, the less I seem to know. What I do know is that my desire to lead a fulfilled life and help others do the same is constant and will never change, and as long as I am learning and growing, I will continue sharing what I've learned so that others can learn and grow too.

> **The more answers I discover, the less I seem to know.**

Reading this book and learning and implementing the seven simple steps I developed to create massive change in your life could be one of the most important things you will ever do.

Whether you just read the steps and learn how to do it conceptually or take the time to work through each step, the most important takeaway I hope you have is that there really is a way to create a plan and make it happen. It doesn't have to be a mystery to find out how to get everything you want out of your life, so my hope is that at a minimum, you walk away with the knowledge that you can take ownership and responsibility whenever you are ready.

# HOW TO USE THIS BOOK

I didn't write this book for entertainment value; although I'm told it can be pretty entertaining.

I wrote it to be an example of what is possible for your own life and for the lives of those you love, and to give clear steps for how to reach for the next level, whatever that looks like.

The best way to make progress is to engage with me. When you're ready, you can go to my website, which is maritautimes.com, for downloadable content, training, and to sign up to receive occasional nuggets in your email inbox.

# PART 1

# My Story: From Teen Mom to CEO

## 1 . 1

# "I'll Just Punch You in the Stomach..."

My boyfriend, Carlos, shared stories with me early on in our relationship about his alcoholic father's explosive temper. He was so violent that his mother would at times place the kids in front of her, which was the only way to stop the blows. His dad had been dead for some years and wasn't able to terrorize the family anymore, and Carlos insisted he would *never* be like his father. I believed him because he chose not to drink or do drugs, played basketball, and was the straight-and-narrow guy of the gang of guys he was always with.

I say "gang," but they weren't an actual gang. They were a group of illegal eighteen to twenty-year-old Mexican nationals who liked hanging around fourteen and fifteen-year-old *gueras* (pronounced "wettas"), which is Spanish slang for "white girls."

I knew this wasn't the right crowd for me, but when I was with them, I felt really alive and grown up. Even more importantly, I felt seen and liked by them, and especially by Carlos, the guy I perceived to be the good guy in the group.

Carlos quickly became my boyfriend. Not long after, we started having sex. It's hard for me to remember if he asked me to or if it was just something I did because I thought I was supposed to. Even though I was only fifteen, these weren't my first sexual experiences. There was no innocence to protect here. He robbed me of nothing.

I went through puberty at nine and, as a result, looked older than I was. I was tall, developed, and *wanted* to be older, like most girls, so I acted how I thought older girls would act. The result was confusing, and I experienced inappropriate attention at nine and ten years of age that quickly turned into sexual abuse by various perpetrators. I eventually ended up losing my virginity at fourteen.

When I missed my period, Carlos gave me twenty dollars for a pregnancy test. I took it at my friend's house in the middle of us dyeing our hair. The positive results were crystal clear almost immediately.

In that instant, my entire world changed. The feeling was so overwhelming that as I walked home, even though I'd only found out minutes earlier, it somehow seemed as though I'd always been

> **In that instant, my entire world changed.**

pregnant. I was searching my mind for a spot to escape to that didn't know this truth for a moment of relief. It was nowhere to be found. It was all-consuming. I felt like my world was closing in on me.

On that walk I made two decisions. The first was that I was going to tell my parents straight away. There was no point in hiding it, and I needed their help.

The second was that I was going to figure this out on my own and not factor Carlos in. I had no question that he was not going to be in the picture. Guys don't stick around in these cases, and it was a waste of time to fantasize anything different.

My parents took the news in stride and, after some discussion, decided not to press charges for statutory rape. I think they figured he was more likely going to be a better help to me not behind bars or deported.

We talked through my options of abortion, adoption, or keeping the baby. It was clear to me that keeping the baby was the only solution for me.

When it came time to share the news with Carlos, his exact words were, "I'll just punch you in the stomach. It's a free abortion."

The look of disgust on my face likely drove him to his next offering of paying for an actual abortion, which he'd already researched and said would be about $500, which I said I would not be doing.

I then let him know I did not expect him to stick around and that I wanted nothing from him. He was angry. He had no control and, maybe worse, he had no leverage. He left and didn't return for a week. When he finally came back, he said that he shared the news with his mom of my pregnancy as well as his offer for me to have an abortion. He told me that she slapped him across the face and told him that he needed to come back and help.

My parents had recently moved us from the Upper Peninsula of Michigan to Arizona and were in the middle of working through some setbacks. With new jobs and no health insurance, I was going to need to get myself on AHCCCS (Arizona Health Care Cost Containment System), Arizona's welfare program. My parents shared with me that getting covered, getting to doctor appointments, and all of the details related to my pregnancy would be 100 percent my responsibility. When the baby came, they would not be babysitting or helping with any sort of childcare either. If I was grown up enough to have sex and get pregnant, I would need to be grown up enough to manage everything myself. They weren't wrong.

I worked to get myself qualified for AHCCCS, but the first time I applied, I was denied. Unlike today, where that can all be done online, I had to find transportation to go apply and fix my errors in person. I would ultimately be denied several times before I finally got the paperwork right.

Fortunately, my doctor (Dr. Mark S. Tong, OBGYN) was willing to see me without payment. My first visit to Dr. Tong to check on the baby was the first pap smear I'd ever had.

Lying on the table feeling completely exposed and terrified, I could feel the tears streaming down my cheeks as he examined me. Thankfully, my mother was there with me.

He was able to help me with everything I needed and provided me with prenatal vitamins at no cost. The only thing we couldn't do was see the baby on a sonogram until I was approved for AHCCCS, which finally happened when I was seven months pregnant.

That's when I learned I would be having a boy. Finally I could start to better picture who this little person was that I was bringing into the world, settle on a name, and start picking out clothes for him. I called Carlos to let him know, and he was elated to learn the baby was going to be a boy.

The next morning, Carlos called at five thirty in the morning. Cell phones weren't a thing yet, so the five thirty a.m. wake-up call to my entire house was a bold move on his part. Even so, it didn't register to me that anything was wrong.

I picked up the phone, and he asked me to meet him outside. I was excited. I thought that he was going to surprise me and take me to breakfast, so I started getting ready, but he got there so fast that I wasn't ready to go when he pulled up. I went out to tell him I needed another minute to get dressed. I was barefoot and in my pj's, and even so, he told me to get in the car. Something was wrong. Having no idea what, I did what he asked, and he immediately put the car in drive. He said nothing.

He drove me to a parking lot at a city park nearby that is not visible from the main road. There was no one there that early in the morning. He parked and then instructed me to get out of the car. The parking lot was bumpy asphalt with loose rocks on it, and it hurt my bare feet to step out on it. At seven months pregnant, I was hovering around 180 lbs. and had swollen feet and ankles, which certainly didn't help.

He started to tell me that he'd been to a party that night, celebrating the news of his boy, where he was told a rumor that I had been with someone else. I had no idea what he was talking about. He accused me of playing dumb, and he started to beat the shit out of me while he yelled at me, called me names, and told me that he didn't know me and that this wasn't his baby. I had not been with anyone else. I kept insisting that it wasn't true, and he continued to punch and kick me wherever he could.

He told me that he never wanted to see me again, and he got in his car to leave. Something came over me, and I got up the guts to yell at him and tell him that he brought me there and he was going to take me home. It was enough for him to let me get back in the car.

He took me home, and I stayed in the car trying to reason with him, telling him that it wasn't true. He got out, opened my passenger door, and forced me out.

I burst through the door of my house sobbing. My parents were furious, but I insisted that they not press charges. I didn't want anything to happen to him. They reluctantly agreed and said that he would not be allowed to see me anymore.

I think we all knew that wasn't going to last, all things considered. He eventually came over to apologize to me and to my parents. I'm guessing that with my due date fast approaching, we all wanted the incident behind us.

My water broke early in the morning on November 15. I shoved a towel between my legs and made my way over to my parents' room, woke my mom up, and told her that it was time. She popped up like a piece of toast, pulled the car around with the trash bag to protect the seat, and we were off.

I called Carlos before we left to let him know we were on our way to the hospital. An hour after we checked in, he still wasn't there. I called again. He'd gone back to sleep. Another hour later, I called again. "Sorry, man, it's just so early." He always said "man" regardless of who he was talking to. English was his second language, and I can't remember if I ever tried to teach him that you don't say that to a woman. That particular time I was especially incensed by it. I was a woman, about to do a thing that only women can do, and he was certainly no man. There was no "man" in this equation.

My parents, thankfully, were there with me, and after I'd been through hours of labor and one failed epidural, he finally walked in, just as they were working on the second epidural.

My beautiful baby boy, Damon Santos Rose, was born that afternoon, and I will never forget the moment I felt him leave my body and then when his warm little perfect body was being laid on my chest. He was such a miracle to me.

An hour or so after delivery, Carlos left to go play basketball. Thankfully, my twin brother, Paul, came and looked after me for several hours as I regained the feeling in my legs and made sense of my new world. I was a mom. Paul was an uncle, and we were only fifteen years old. It was a lot to take in, and he made sure I wasn't alone while my parents went home to rest.

In the hospital, I completed all of the paperwork, including the information for Damon's birth certificate. I did not put Carlos on it. I was trying to think into the future and was afraid he would have the ability to take our child to Mexico if things went sideways with us.

## The Reality of Being a Single Mom

One month later, I turned sixteen.

The next two years can only be described as survival from one day to the next. Carlos did not live with us and was never there to help.

My parents stayed true to their word that they, too, would not be helping to watch the baby. They provided everything Damon and I needed and had just one stipulation. They made it clear that if they were buying diapers, they were going to be cloth diapers. If I didn't want that, they told me I would need to go to work to buy my own diapers.

Off to work I went.

Before I had Damon, I'd worked for my dad, helping to put insurance application kits together and cleaning the office. He didn't have enough work for me for even twenty hours a week, so I started my first real job working at Ross when Damon was just a few weeks old. The manager hiring me was concerned about my health and ability to work with such a new little person at home. It meant a lot to me that he cared, but I insisted I would be fine.

I started to develop a wicked rash on my arms and legs, and when I went to the doctor for it, he said that I was so fatigued that my immune system was compromised. Basic things my body could normally keep in check were now causing issues for me. He recommended letting go of the job until the baby was a little older and instead just focusing on our care.

I made two phone calls that day. The first was to my manager to quit my job, and the second was to Carlos. I called him and told him that I was so tired after weeks of little to no sleep and reminded him that my parents were sticking to their guns about not helping with the baby. I cried and I told him I needed to sleep for one night. Just *one night* if he could take the baby or ask his mom for help so that I could sleep.

He laughed at me and told me that I was the one that wanted to have the baby, and I was the one that insisted I could do it all on my own, so here was my chance.

I was so angry I threw the phone at the wall so hard that it broke into pieces.

Such an asshole. *And* he was right—I said I could do this on my own, and there I was. That was what alone looked like.

At eight weeks old, Damon could go to daycare paid for by the Department of Economic Security, and I could go to school and work without the need to arrange a sitter. I went back to school and was able to get a job as a cashier at the Flamingo Car Wash on weekends, where my boss paid me $4.25 an hour under the table and let me bring Damon to work with me.

Wanting to graduate on time, I was taking additional early-morning classes to catch myself up from the time I took off to have the baby, which I eventually did. I was also able to fit in one more season of basketball, which I'd been playing since the sixth grade.

My boss at the car wash was the first and only verbally abusive boss I have ever had. He treated every single person like trash, from the ticket writers to the migrant workers to us, the cashiers. I guess I can give him credit for being an equal opportunity asshole.

So when I was approached with a receptionist job offer by one of the managers of a car dealership that came in regularly to wash cars, it was an easy yes.

After a year of maintaining a full schedule of school and work with irregular sleep, I ended up really sick with the flu. It was my first (and I pray last) experience with this kind of flu. Body aches, fever, and cold chills, two trips to the ER, and an eventual diagnosis of pleurisy in my lungs, which meant every single breath I took hurt. I could feel where my lungs stopped and started in my body. I literally thought I was going to die.

After two weeks of this illness and managing Damon's care alone, I started to finally recover and knew I needed to make a change. Reluctant to let anything go in my schedule, I decided I would try again to get help.

I couldn't get Carlos to watch the baby at his house. The only way I *might* get help would be if he lived with us and was just immersed in the environment. So that was my genius idea. Move him in, and then I'll finally have a partner to help me.

My parents weren't keen on the idea and told me that the only way that could happen is if we were engaged to be married. I didn't want to marry him; I just wanted his help. He and I agreed we were not on a path for marriage. But he went and bought a cheap ring to appease my parents, and Carlos moved in.

Instead of help, what I quickly realized was that I now had two babies in the house instead of one. I knew his mother did *everything* for him, but it didn't occur to me that he would expect the same from me.

One afternoon, as I was pushing the vacuum with my right hand and holding the baby on my hip with my left, Carlos, who was seated at the end of the bed watching TV, yelled for me over the vacuum, "Mari! *Mari!*" I thought something was wrong. I turned off the vacuum and looked at him, concerned. "Yes?" I asked. "I'm thirsty," he said. I looked at him, cocked my head, squinted my eyes, and said, "You know where the kitchen is." I knew "them's fightin' words," and I didn't care.

15

He got up and got in my face as though he was going to hit me. I didn't flinch. Not because I was tough but because I knew he wouldn't hit me. My dad was just down the hall.

I was seventeen, he was twenty-three, and Damon was two. It was clear to me that nothing was ever going to change, so I immediately bagged up his clothes in two black trash bags and asked my dad to drive him home.

I remember crying *so hard* watching the car drive away. It hurt so much, but I knew it was the right move. We were officially done.

After that, Carlos told me in no uncertain terms that I was never to ask for help with the baby from him or anyone in his family. Which, of course, was already the case, but it was his only leverage, so I guess he decided it was time to reiterate it.

Months later there was a work party being thrown, and I was invited. Like any other eighteen-year-old, I wanted to spread my new "adult" wings and felt like I should be able to go.

I called Carlos' sister Janet and asked her if she or her mom could watch the baby for a couple of hours so I could go. She agreed. We both knew I was entering the danger zone with this request, but Carlos and I weren't together anymore, and I told myself that time was enough to get him to calm down, and he was being unreasonable. But I knew I was pushing it.

When I returned to pick Damon up, all the lights in the house were off. I gently knocked on the front door, and it immediately opened. Carlos' face emerged from the dark. He stepped out and closed the door behind him. He was *furious*. He got in my face, said words that I can't remember now, and the next thing I knew, I was being held against the wall by my neck. He was choking me and told me to never leave the baby there again.

Message received.

# Moving into a Brighter Future—but How?

I got back to my life and made my peace with the fact that I was still and would always be 100 percent on my own.

School was going really well. Having Damon switched my brain and my motivation on, and I genuinely wanted to learn and succeed. Before that, I wasn't very academically inclined and was even tested at one point to determine if I had special needs. I just couldn't understand, retain, or focus when it came to learning.

I had a purpose now, though, and it seemed to help me focus. My purpose was that I did not want Damon or me to become just another statistic in the history of teen pregnancies. I knew we could do better, and I was officially on a mission to make that happen.

Even though I had this mission, and I'd caught myself up on school, I felt like school was just taking entirely too long. Sure, the finish line of graduation was around the corner, but then what? Another four-plus years of college and financial hardship while incurring a ton of debt without even knowing what I actually wanted to do for a living when I "grew up"? It just didn't feel like the right option for me. There had to be a better way.

When I learned that I could receive a high school diploma equivalent (a GED) in less time and could start working full time, I convinced my parents that was the best move and dropped out.

I received my GED the same year I would have graduated, and life went right on. To this day, not once have I been asked for proof of my diploma or equivalency, which was my biggest fear when making that decision. I was afraid that someone would ask, and I would have the "loser" version.

It's not the loser version, and no one gives a shit. It's definitely nothing like walking across the stage or the full high school experience, but that's not going to be the path for everyone, and that's OK.

My dad was in the process, at the time, of buying the insurance agency he'd been working in. The agency was called A Best Brokerage and was located in a small house converted into an office in Central Phoenix and was a long-term care insurance (LTCI) and Medicare supplement insurance brokerage.

My dad told me that if I was able to be a receptionist at the car dealership, why not come and do it for the agency? Made sense to me.

When I started with the company, there were no computers, and our product supplies were housed in a makeshift shelf over the bathtub in the bathroom. There were more than a few awkward moments when an agent would come in to pick up supplies, and we had to wait for someone to get out of the bathroom to get them.

Still, it was our office, and we were proud of it. My twin brother, Paul, also started working with the company full time, and when my dad upgraded to computers, Paul and I were tasked with entering all of the data from our paper files into a database.

From that point forward, I was responsible for checking the status of insurance cases that were pending in underwriting, noting the files, and informing the insurance agents that wrote them of the updates.

I loved my job. I loved typing. I loved learning about the medical histories of clients and working with the agents.

My dad also recruited my mom away from a teaching position she was working in to help, and he also hired a friend of his, Anton Byers. He later hired Anton's fiancé, Sierra, too.

Sierra and Anton became our managers, and both were very invested in helping Paul and me grow personally and professionally. They taught us how to speak and dress more professionally (picture spaghetti straps and jeans before that), and they inspected every document we sent out of the company for spelling and grammar.

I shared with Anton once that I wanted to know as much as I could about *everything*. Specifically, I never wanted to look or feel dumb in a conversation because I was in the dark about a particular subject. He recommended that I start listening to National Public Radio (NPR) as a starting point for learning and broadening my understanding of the world around me.

> I shared with Anton once that I wanted to know as much as I could about *everything*.

I turned on 91.5 (KJZZ), our local NPR station, and started to listen daily to and from work instead of Darude, Destiny's Child, and Dr. Dre.

Like a lot of eighteen-year-olds, I had a bumpin' sound system in my car. My music had the power to fill me with energy and inspiration and gave me a feeling like I was a badass that could do anything. To go from that to talk radio was rough.

When I made the switch, the very first story that was on was about current events in Israel. I remember it because I remember how hard it was for me to understand what they were talking about. It was a weird experience to understand the language but not understand what they were saying.

Very quickly, I felt dumb and overwhelmed by what I didn't know. I realized from there that I didn't even know what was going on in Phoenix, let alone our state, country, or our world. I experienced literal physical discomfort. It was exactly the feeling I was trying to avoid, which was my cue that I was on the right track.

Over time as I listened, my language and speaking ability began to further develop. I would practice and try on words the journalists were using, and the exposure to a broad sampling of subjects from both the news and other journalism opened me up to a richer, deeper understanding of the world around me. It gave me access to the human experience beyond my own reality and helped me to get outside of myself. I even started listening on the weekends and was introduced to more entertaining but also informative shows like *Car Talk*; *The Motley Fool*; *Wait Wait … Don't Tell Me*; and *A Prairie Home Companion.*

NPR became my constant companion and was my launchpad into my lifelong journey of self-education.

## 1.2

# In an Instant, My Brother Was Gone

When I was a kid, we moved a lot. People always think "army" when I say that, but anyone who is a PK (pastor's kid) also typically experiences a childhood where moving is normal every one to two years.

The hardest move we faced as kids was from Ontonagon, a small town in the Upper Peninsula of Michigan (population 1,200) to Mesa, Arizona—a suburb of Phoenix, where our school had almost as many students and teachers in it as the town we'd moved from. Paul and I were thirteen, and our older brother David was sixteen.

David hated it so much that my parents agreed to let him go back to Michigan to stay with friends to finish high school there. After graduating in '96, he moved back to Arizona and lived with us for a short time before enlisting in the army.

He went through basic training in Aberdeen, Maryland, and was later stationed in South Korea, which he loved. He then finished out his service at Fort Carson, Colorado, and was honorably discharged in July of 2000.

The army returned to us a much more grown-up version of my brother. Before that he had a pretty bad temper and fought a lot with my dad and brother, Paul. But now, he was calm, mature, and helpful.

He set up his computer and taught us about AOL, which had email and messaging. It was the coolest thing to check in from time to time to hear, "You've got mail," after, of course, the painful (but now amusing and nostalgic) sounds of dial-up.

While David was traveling the world, Paul and I were growing up too. By this time, we both had two years under our belt in the family business; Paul was in a serious, committed relationship; and I was a single mom raising Damon, who was then three. We had all moved out, and we all happened to move back home at about the same time. My parents owned a large ranch-style house, and there was plenty of room, so much so that even Damon had his own room.

David drove a motorcycle, the racing kind that can go from zero to sixty in 2.3 seconds type of bike. He'd been out partying one night and called to let me know he was going to stay put for the evening instead of trying to drive home.

When the doorbell rang at ten a.m. the next morning, I thought it was David messing with me or that maybe he'd lost his key.

Expecting to see his face when I opened the door, I was surprised to instead be greeted by two men. One was a police officer, and one was in plain clothes. They had a look on their face that I can't describe, and they asked for Mary Rose, my mom.

I was the only one home.

I quickly made some calculations in my head and realized that if I told them she wasn't there, I might not get the information about why they were there. I had to know why they were there.

My mother and I share the same name, Mary Rose. I hadn't spelled mine with a *y* since the first grade, when I wanted to be different from my mom and my grandma who both had the same name, but they didn't need to know that. So with complete honesty, I said, "I am Mary Rose." They looked at each other a little confused, looked back at me, and asked if they could come inside. I let them in, and they asked, "Is there someplace we can sit down?"

My heart began to race as I walked them over to the living room only steps away. My head felt like it was floating like a balloon. I didn't feel like I was in my body anymore. Everything started to move in slow motion.

I sat on one side of the room; the officer and the man in plain clothes sat on the other. "We're sorry to inform you that David was killed this morning in a motorcycle accident on the 101 freeway and McKellips." That's all I remember them saying.

The words sank in. The fact that these two men were sitting in our living room sank in. The fact that David wasn't home yet sank in. Maybe it wasn't David; maybe it was someone else. But then why would they be here? How would they know to ask for my mom? That was the freeway exit to my aunt's house, where he'd been the night before. It had to be David.

I stood up thinking I was about to throw up, and then I started to cry. It all just continued to sink in a little deeper into my head, into my heart, and into my body.

Then it occurred to me that I didn't know when he died. "What time did he die?" I asked.

"Six thirty this morning," one of them responded. I looked at the time. He had been dead for four hours, and somehow I didn't know. I didn't feel anything. How could I not have felt *something*?

"*My parents*! I have to tell my parents!" I couldn't let another minute go by without telling them. They couldn't go on living without

23

the knowledge that they were now living in a world that their son was no longer in. "I have to call my dad."

I picked up the black cordless house phone and dialed my dad's cell phone number. He always answered; I knew I could count on that. And he almost always answered saying, "Hellooooo," in a funny, playful way. That day was no different. It made my task even more painful. There wasn't any way to sugarcoat anything, and being nineteen, I lacked the capacity to brace him in any way for what I had to say. I was crying, and I said into the phone, "Dad, David's dead. He died this morning." I threw the phone down so that I couldn't hear my dad's response. I couldn't bear it. But it didn't matter. I could hear him anyway.

> As I watched, I realized that this was one of those things that people go through that changes their lives forever.

My next memory is being in the back seat of the counselor's car on my way to be with my parents and Paul at the office. Sitting there, I left my head and heart, and I began to escape into what felt like a movie. I felt removed from it, like I was watching a story play out in front of me. But it wasn't someone else's story. It was our story.

As I watched, I realized that this was one of those things that people go through that changes their lives forever. It happens to everyone at some point, and it was now happening to us. To my family. It was our turn.

The date was August 28, 2000. My brother was twenty-three.

# The Epiphany: Which Road to Follow?

After David's funeral, things went pretty dark in my life. My parents decided to sell the house we were all living in, and I found a condo to rent in Old Town Scottsdale.

I smoked at the time, and I started smoking twice as much. I started drinking earlier and earlier every day that I wasn't working, and then even if I was working, along with various other self-destructive activities. I was trying to kill pain but feel things at the same time. I wanted to be left alone, but I also craved connection.

Sitting in my darkness and self-pity, I was somehow struck with an epiphany. If David's life could end just like that, in just one instant, mine could too. I started to feel panicked and began to experience a sense of urgency about my life and my time here.

In that moment I went from this perspective that I have my entire life ahead of me to figure things out to feeling like I'd better hurry up and live and get it all in, because the worst thing ever would be to die not ever knowing what I could have done.

I started to look ahead to my future and think about what I wanted to be able to say about my life. I could see two clear paths ahead of me.

The first road represented the path I was on, and it ended with me having few or no teeth, overweight, disease ridden, and nothing to show for my life.

The second path was unclear, but I could see where it ended. It had healthy relationships, financial security, self-confidence, and abundance. I knew I wanted all of those things for my life, and I didn't see any reason why I didn't deserve it or couldn't figure out how to get it.

I knew that I wasn't going to be able to figure it out on my own. If I could have, I already would have. I decided to get help. I found my Blue Cross & Blue Shield card, flipped it over, and got connected with a counselor. I was pretty sure that within a few sessions, I would have it all figured out.

# 1.3

# Time Bombs

My counselor was Tamara Rounds, MSW, LCSW. Our first meeting was exactly as I expected. She was warm, smart, and she had a quiet confidence about her that I admired. I felt like she saw me and that she cared about me.

I dressed as perfectly as I could and tried to present myself as a person who had it all together, which made no sense considering I was there to dish out all of my problems.

She asked questions, and I answered. I then shared with her that I'd had a series of incredibly unhealthy relationships, I struggled with my self-esteem, and I was certain I was broadcasting some sort of message that said, "I'm a doormat; feel free to use me." At the time, my priority was working on me so that I could attract a better relationship, because I was pretty sure if I had the perfect relationship, that would lead to the perfect life.

> **I'd never told anyone, but if anyone was going to understand, it would be her.**

We were nearing the end of the appointment, and I knew there was one more thing that I had to tell her, but I was so filled with shame. I'd never told anyone, but if anyone was going to understand, it would be her.

I told her that I had been sexually abused or assaulted from the time I was nine into my late teens by various perpetrators. As an adult, the abuse was simply converted to unhealthy relationships that lacked boundaries. The shame was a genuine belief that it happened because of things that I did or that I didn't do, but either way, I'd brought it on myself.

The abuse started shortly after my first period that started when I was in third grade. I began to develop and look like a sixteen-year-old by the time I was ten, but I was just a little girl stuck in a young woman's body, and I didn't know what to do with it or about it. I got a lot of attention from older boys as well as men, which felt great, but the things they said to me didn't. But I liked the attention. It was really confusing.

My counselor looked at me and said with total empathy and compassion that normally, with something like that, she would ask me to come back the next day and would work me in. However, she was leaving for vacation and wouldn't be able to see me for two weeks.

I felt like Bob Wiley in the movie *What About Bob?* when Dr. Marvin tells him after their first session that he's going on vacation for the summer.

While I wasn't an almost-paralyzed, multiphobic personality that was in a constant state of panic like Bob Wiley, I did unearth a lot of stuff that we brought right up to the surface. I realized I was going to have to sit with it for a couple of weeks without guidance. "I'm fine! I'll be fine."

That afternoon, I went to my parents' house and slept for what felt like three days. I guess it was a bigger deal than I thought.

# Moving into a Life I Could Create Myself

The long, hard road of therapy began. We made excellent progress over the years, and I just kept facing things head-on as they came up, thinking and hoping that with each next session, I would have it all figured out.

What I was working toward was a bright, new future that didn't resemble anything close to my past. It was working, and I was becoming the kind of person that had the potential to attract healthier relationships and maintain healthy boundaries.

At twenty-one, my parents shared some life insurance funds of David's that I used to buy a small townhome that was perfect for my then-six-year-old and me.

My home life was stable, and our business was beginning to grow. We changed our name from A Best Brokerage to Western Asset Protection (WAP), rebranded, and relocated to a more respectable office space.

My skills as an administrative assistant had begun to evolve, and at twenty-two, I gained more experience with the LTCI products and began to help agents design coverage plans and help them with underwriting. Wanting to gain further knowledge and credibility, I also obtained my Long-Term Care Professional designation.

With my increased confidence, I started offering product training classes, thinking that would be more efficient than the many one-to-one calls it took for me to communicate to agents. Each session went great, and I was developing my skills as a speaker and trainer, but I was always met with questions about overcoming objections to the product and other questions that required sales experience.

Selling long-term care insurance is hard. The coverage is expensive, hard to qualify for, and it's a subject most people never want to think or talk about. I had zero experience with how to deal with common objections nor did I understand how to help the client evaluate affordability and coverage limits based on their specific financial circumstances.

At that time, we were fortunate to meet Bryan Herdt, who was a top-producing agent who had been professionally trained at Genworth Financial.

He agreed to come work with us to help us develop our LTCI sales program. He shared an office with me, which meant I would be fully immersed in learning what he knew.

Bryan was brilliant in both sales and training. The first thing he had me do was read the book *Integrity Selling* by Ron Willingham, which I did, and then I went through his sales training program. He taught us (a handful of our agents and me) how to call on leads and set appointments. I learned how to prequalify over the phone and how to design the best plans based on the answers to their health and wealth questions. It was outstanding, and it gave me the confidence to start selling myself.

In my first month, I wrote $30K in LTCI premium and felt like I finally understood everything I needed to know to best help our agents. I was twenty-three years old and the least likely person to be advising people on their elder care insurance preparation coverage options, but the system gave me borrowed confidence until I had enough experience to have it naturally. I followed the process, and it worked.

Across the street from our office was a gym. I had quit smoking and drinking and was working out there regularly, including running on the treadmill, something I'd never done before but found to be therapeutic. My confidence grew, and I started signing up for races and loved the competition. I would pick one runner off at a time (meaning I would get ahead of them) and would eventually place in my category in many of the races that I ran in.

It was time for Damon to start sports, too, so I signed him up for soccer through the city of Phoenix. His first practice with this team was on a hot June summer day in 2003, when he was still just six.

Coach Andy was tall and so handsome, with an athletic build and pitch-black, thick hair. He had distinguishing thick, black eyebrows, almond eyes, and a perfect smile. Yes, we were there for soccer … but *yay*! The coach was cute too.

He was a really great coach to the kids and seemed like a good father to his son Andres, who was also on the team and the same age as Damon. He was patient, he was kind, and he was also a little tough on them in all the right ways.

We became fast friends, and I was *so* disappointed to learn that he was dating someone, but then again, so was I.

I ended my relationship, and he eventually ended his, but we didn't immediately begin to date. That wasn't the obvious next step. In fact, I wasn't even sure if he was actually interested in me.

Finally, after two years of friendship, he asked me on a date. At least I thought it was a date, but it was hard to tell. It wasn't like anything else we'd done together. It was dinner. We were going somewhere nice. We were getting dressed up. While we always hung out and did stuff, we'd never done anything like that.

It was such a big deal to me that I asked my best friend, Christi Anne, to come over and help me with my makeup. I didn't wear makeup at the time and wanted my makeup, hair, and dress to make it crystal clear that for me, this was a date, just in case he thought we were just being friends again. He showed up dressed to impress, too, and that's when I knew we were on the same page.

It turned out he'd been nuts about me since the day we met, but as big and strong as he was, he was also painfully shy. He later told me he was nervous around me all the time. I had no idea.

We dated for two years, and then he asked me to marry him on my twenty-sixth birthday in December of 2006. We married four months later on April 14, 2007.

Things were shaping up for my life. I had this amazing man who adored me and who I was madly in love with and attracted to, and he was a wonderful father to our boys. We renovated and then sold the townhome and bought my parents' house that had a pool and everything we needed.

Everything was going great—except for the small detail that going into our wedding, we were barely scraping by financially. I wasn't great at managing the finances, and I struggled to get Andrew to plan and work on it with me. We ended up using most of the money we received at our wedding to just keep ourselves afloat. Part of me hopes that none of my family reads this book. It's literally one of the greatest points of shame for me in my adult life.

It was humiliating to me, even though no one knew. We had no debt, but we were also barely making ends meet and had no savings. We were living on the edge.

Two weeks after our wedding, while playing tennis, I realized that a part of my vision was gone. If I looked straight ahead, there was only darkness in the peripheral vision on the left side of my right eye.

I stopped playing and called my regular vision doctor, who instructed me to call a specialist immediately. I had an appointment later that afternoon and was on the table the next day to have surgery for a detached retina. Not having surgery immediately could cause permanent vision loss. It was an easy decision, and I didn't ask many questions.

With some surgery history under my belt, I wasn't too concerned. I checked in, put my gown on, and lay down on the bed. They took my blood pressure, and it was fine. An anesthesiologist came in and said that he'd be giving me a twilight medication to do a block on my eye of some sort. Sounded good to me.

The next thing I knew, I was waking up while being wheeled into surgery. I panicked. I said, "Um … I'm awake!" The person wheeling me in said, "Yes, you are going to be awake for this procedure. We can't do general anesthesia for eye surgeries."

*Whaaaat the … No. No, no, no, no, no, no, no! This can't be. OK. Calm down … I've been through tougher stuff than this. I've had other surgeries. Calm down. Breathe. Relax. (Still being wheeled in) … Wait, what is this?* (It was the first time I noticed that my face was completely covered.) *It's blue; I can't see anything at all.*

"What is this on my face?" I asked. Someone responded that it was a face covering to create a surgical field. This surgical field thing was literally stuck to the rest of my face with an adhesive, leaving only an opening for my right eye.

I was claustrophobic at the time, and as a teenager, I had constant, debilitating panic attacks that started when we moved from Michigan to Arizona, and I could feel one coming on. I had to think. I had to calm down and think.

I had to have the surgery, or I would go blind in my right eye. I pulled myself together and lay there in horror as I saw instruments in my eye from the inside out throughout the surgery. I was given Versed, which I am certain is what got me through it, but it wasn't enough. Anything other than "completely knocked out" just isn't enough for something like that.

After what felt like an eternity, they finally wheeled me into recovery and called Andrew in. I couldn't speak. I had no words. My

33

body and my brain were just stuck in a holding position as I tried to process and cope with what had just happened.

My doctor came to check on me. He was the coldest, most unkind and uncommunicative doctor I'd ever had. I never wanted to see his face again.

When Andrew packed me up in the car to take me home, I started to cry. The stuck started to finally come unstuck, and I told him that this was absolutely the worst thing that I had ever been through.

When a person has a detached retina, the surgery performed is called a vitrectomy. I won't describe it here, and if you are squeamish, don't look it up. The ending to that surgery story is that a gas bubble is installed in the eyeball, and the patient must lie facedown for two weeks so that the bubble can rise up and press on the retina to help readhere it to the back wall of the eye.

My mom came over with a massage table so that I could comfortably lie facedown for the two weeks ahead. She equipped me with a mirror so that I could watch my favorite network, Investigation Discovery, for the coming weeks.

After getting me settled on the massage table, she went downstairs to crack open a bottle of wine for us. Before I joined her, I needed to take a quick pregnancy test. We'd stopped my birth control just before the wedding so we could start trying to get pregnant. The test was thankfully positive! We toasted in celebration, my glass with water, hers with wine. And then I lay facedown. For two weeks.

## An Eventful Pregnancy

Five months into my pregnancy, my retina redetached in my right eye, and we were going to have to do another vitrectomy. This time I did some research on doctors and found one who had a much better bedside manner.

He said the first doctor did a good job on my surgery but that it detached again because the first doctor was likely trying to avoid touching the lens of my eye, which would have caused a cataract. In his effort to not touch the lens, he missed a part of the retina in the surgery.

My new doctor would be touching the lens to make sure he got all of it this time, and he was also going to install a scleral buckle to the bottom of my eye, which would reshape it to prevent future detachments.

He explained that this would certainly cause a cataract and that he would not be the doctor to operate on that, and also that I would not be able to have that procedure done until after I delivered the baby.

He also helped me understand why this was happening, which was helpful. He told me I have a condition called lattice degeneration, which meant that because of the shape of my eyes, my retina is stretched thin, and if the slightest hole occurs, it will allow the fluid in the eye to make its way in and cause the retina to peel off like wallpaper peeling off a wall.

I had the second vitrectomy, and while it was crappy, it was at least far less traumatic. I had to recover for two weeks lying facedown in bed, but only on my side because I couldn't lie on my stomach while I was five months pregnant.

Four months later, on January 6, 2008, after a smooth

> **We adjusted to our new life that shifted quickly from only being Damon and me to a family of five all together in our new home.**

35

pregnancy (aside from two detached retinas), our beautiful baby girl, Sophie Isabel Tautimes, was born.

We adjusted to our new life that shifted quickly from only being Damon and me to a family of five all together in our new home. We wrapped up the eyeball stuff after a few more procedures (lasered the left eye retina that was showing signs of future issues, cataract surgery on the right, and then another laser surgery after the cataract surgery to clear off scar tissue on the lens). We were finally on our way to peace and lifelong happiness.

## The Financial Issues Hit

Except there was still that one thing. We barely had our nose out of the water financially before the wedding, and now, with the eye surgeries, pregnancy, and related medical expenses, we were officially underwater and began accumulating debt just to make ends meet.

We had another issue, too, which was that when we originally bought the house, I had this ridiculous assumption that if the bank told us we could afford it and helped us find a way to make it work, that it meant we could actually afford it. Deep down I knew better.

The loan we signed on for was an adjustable-rate mortgage, which meant our payments were fixed for the initial term but would then go up in the future. It made it so that we could get into the house, but it didn't mean that we would be able to afford to stay there. I justified that our income would continue to rise, and we would be OK. Or maybe that was the story the mortgage broker sold me. Either way, I was the one responsible for making the decision in the end, and I made the wrong one.

We could not afford the home we were living in, and I kept burying the truth in credit cards and loans, and before I knew it, my credit card payments were so high that I couldn't afford to make the payments.

About this time, Andrew was in a minor car accident caused by the other party that totaled our vehicle. State Farm went after the other insurance company and paid us $19K within a few days of the accident.

The other vehicle we had at the time was a two-door 1996 VW Golf GTI that was Andrew's commuter car, and the family simply did not fit in that. We decided to visit a Honda dealership with our insurance money in hand and walked out with a shiny, brand-new, sexy black Honda Pilot that was far more suitable for a growing family.

The car payment, however, was not suitable for *our* growing family. It was more than anything I'd ever paid for a car before.

With this new payment, I felt more loyal to the car payment than the past debts I'd incurred and stopped making payments on the other debts to try to make this one work.

Late payment notices were always in the mail. It became the new standard, but I never got used to it.

It was when I received my first certified mail from the credit card company about a court date for unpaid debt that I started to realize I couldn't run from this anymore. Everything was officially catching up to us.

Looking at our options, I learned about short selling the house. I was able to get us out easily and with very little pain, and I figured with the savings from not having a mortgage payment, if we lived with Andrew's parents for six months, we could create a plan, pay down our debt, and get back on our feet.

His parents were most gracious to let us stay with them, but it was demoralizing to me. *All* of it was, and my brilliant "we'll pay down our debts" plan was just not happening. I could not fix our situation, and instead of working on that, the only thing I could think about every single day was getting us our own place. I felt like once we could get into a better and more dignified home of our own, we could start to work together on a plan.

We found an apartment on Central that was bright with lots of windows, next to the pool, across the street from the park and light rail, and it was affordable. We loved it. From this inspiring and independent place, I was sure we could solve our problems.

At about the same time, things in my family business were becoming increasingly challenging. While I was working on buying a house, getting married, eyeball issues, pregnancy, and then my newborn, our company was growing, and fast.

We had taken on new Medicare Advantage and prescription drug plans a few years earlier and it was taking off, so my brother Paul's focus transitioned to that full time along with my dad's.

We partnered with a local agency that offered life insurance, disability income, and annuities for financial planners. They wanted to offer LTCI too, and I agreed to become their LTCI Department. I had two phones on my desk, one for them and one for our agency. Overnight we went from being in just Arizona to adding about twenty new states, each with its own approved version of products that I needed to quickly learn both product and agent licensing and continuing education for.

I also decided I would become a Continuing Education (CE) trainer as a way to meet the needs of our existing agent base and also as a way to attract more agents. It was a mandatory training, and I knew it would give us exposure to a whole new audience of insurance agents and financial planners.

# A State of Overwhelm

Hungry to keep learning and growing, I didn't realize that I'd been piling on more and more and was now managing marketing, communications, quoting and underwriting prequalification, new business, case status, sales and product training, and now CE training on top of multistate expansion. I took four weeks off for my maternity leave and went back as fast as I could. In between calls I would race to pump my milk. Andrew and I talked about giving Sophie the best and that I would nurse her for six months before putting her on the bottle. I would sit in a small, dark office in the back and pump. And cry. And pump. And watch my milk supply decrease, and then I'd cry about that. I would talk to Andrew about weaning her at just two months in, but he insisted because we'd agreed that I needed to keep trying.

Instead, I just quit nursing her and just didn't even talk with him about it. I had no choice. Something had to give, and nursing the baby was the thing.

I needed help, and I really wanted more time with my baby, but at the same time, I felt like I should be able to do all of it. I did ask for help and maternity leave, but it wasn't in the budget. My dad and my brother were each working a lot more hours than I was able to, and I felt like I wasn't doing my part or doing enough. I felt like I just needed to get my shit together and suck it up.

It didn't occur to me at the time, though, that I was comparing myself to my dad and brother, who had each other to back the other one up, no kids, and the ability to work uninterrupted and for long hours.

I was also the parent on call for the kids if they were sick, had a bloody nose and needed a change of clothes, or if the classroom needed a volunteer. Unlike them, my days weren't open-ended to just work; they were sandwiched with getting the kids to/from school, meals, homework, and after-school activities.

Knowing I could be called away at any time, fitting in times to pump my milk in between tasks/calls/meetings, I had to be as efficient as I possibly could with the short bursts of focus that I had, and 100 percent of the time, I felt like I was under the gun and needed to press hard and fast. And I did. I could get done in four hours what it might take someone else eight hours to do. I was crazy efficient, but it was still never enough. I needed help.

At home, I would meal plan and prepare dinners for our family as often as I could. I wanted to be a good wife and mom and do the things that good wives and moms do. But I needed help there too. I finally got up the guts to ask Andrew for help. I asked him if he thought he might be able to do the dishes, since I made dinner. And then if maybe some nights he might be able to make dinner, at which point I would do the dishes. Also, if he could help with some meal planning and grocery shopping too.

He had a mom who was fortunate to be able to stay at home and made everything look so easy. It just didn't make sense to him why I couldn't just do the same.

He looked at me across the kitchen and told me that the dishes were easy: just put them in the dishwasher. What was the big deal? And meal planning? What is that? Just buy the groceries you need and make food. "It's not that hard." He walked away.

If I ever pushed back, it resulted in automatic silent treatment, anywhere from one to three days long, depending on the seriousness of the argument. At the end of the silence, he would extend some sort of olive branch, and I would be so relieved to be reconnecting that I just let whatever the issue was go.

Except, it wasn't really letting go. It was just burying it down deep.

He had the same attitude about the finances. "It's not that hard, Mari. There's money coming in, and there are bills that need to be paid going out. Just pay the bills."

I did convince him at one point to attend a class by Dave Ramsey called Financial Peace University, which was really great. We learned some excellent things and enjoyed the classes, but knowledge isn't power. Action is power, and we still could not get on the same page about taking action.

> According to the most important people in my life...I should be able to do all of this, and the issue was with me.

I struggled desperately to manage it all and even attended FranklinCovey workshops to learn how to manage my time and priorities better. I was certain that there was something wrong with me. Because according to the most important people in my life, those who loved me the most and who I loved and wanted to please the most, I should be able to do all of this, and the issue was with me.

## Why Can't I Do It All?

Every single day, I was failing both at work and at home. No matter how hard I tried, how fast I worked, how many things I got done, there was always a mountain ahead to be done. I felt lower than whale shit. Every. Single. Day.

Facing absolute exhaustion and tired of feeling like a failure, I broke. I needed to let something go. I couldn't let go of my family, so I decided to let go of my position in our business and go into LTCI sales full time instead. I figured this way, I would have more flexibility to get more done, and I could start feeling better about my time with my family.

I gave my dad and brother two months to find a replacement for me. They eventually hired an entry-level receptionist and handed her my duties. Because that's the level of skill and talent they perceived it took to do my job. It was offensive and hurtful, but it wasn't my issue anymore. It was also affirmation that we were not going to be on the same page anytime soon about what it took to do my job.

What I was either not aware of or didn't take advice on was that when a person goes into a 100 percent commission sales position, they need to have at least six to twelve months in financial reserves, if not more, until their commissions and residuals begin to build up. They also needed resources for marketing and basic business expenses, like a computer, database, business cards, and filing for an LLC. I was going into this with even less than zero dollars in the bank.

That year, I made less than $20K in sales before taxes, and between that and Andrew's income, we still didn't have quite enough to cover our bills or answer our debts.

Our VW Golf GTI had broken down and was going to cost $1,500 to fix. We were down to the Honda Pilot, which I used to take Andrew and the boys to/from work and school, and the boys were also to take public transit.

I'd called my dad, defeated and crying, to tell him how hard it was and asked to borrow money because our account was overdrawn, and I needed to buy groceries. He told me I was welcome to come back to work, and I told him it just wasn't an option. I couldn't live like that anymore either. I was going to have to figure it out.

My parents would come over and put groceries in my cupboards and gave me money to help us get through to the next paycheck. Not being able to put food on the table for my children was a visceral experience. Scarcity was so great that I could not see a path out. The same vision that had carried me through in times past was not available to me. I was officially in survival mode.

## From Private to Public Transit

At that point, it was clear that keeping the Pilot was no longer a priority. It didn't take priority over feeding our family. I called the dealership to see if they would take the Honda Pilot back and wipe the debt clean. They said to bring it in, so while Andrew was at work and the boys were at school, I packed Sophie up in her car seat, and we drove to the dealership. I had to write them a check for one hundred dollars. I have no idea what for—a restocking fee? I was happy to pay it so that I could recapture $500+ a month in our budget.

The employee at the dealership was very gracious and thankfully didn't ask questions. He offered to take us home, saving me from needing to take public transit. I accepted. There was no small talk. It was awkward for us both. I cried in the back seat sitting with my baby, who thankfully wasn't old enough to have any idea what was going on.

The way I notified Andrew about my decision to turn us into a family with no car was to take the train with Sophie down to his work. When he walked out and asked where we parked, I told him we were on the train, and he knew what it meant. We rode the train home in silence, and not a word was ever said about it again. For our family of five, public transit was our new form of transportation.

I was still managing to book new LTCI clients all things considered, and one morning I met with an accountant at his office, where his wife joined us to talk about their options for long-term care coverage.

After reviewing their options, they picked their plan and then wrote me a check for $7,000, which was going to cover their combined first-year annual premium. At that time, they were paying for memory care for just one of their parents in a nursing home at $10,000 a month; by comparison, paying the annual premium was a no-brainer for them.

As we neared the end of the appointment, he told his wife that they would be able to go to lunch together if she had time. Thank God she did, because I wasn't sure how I was going to make my way to the bus stop without him seeing me. The parking lot and street were visible from his office. I hung back while they went to their car to leave, and once I knew the coast was clear, I made my way to the bus stop. They would certainly have canceled that check had they seen me getting onto a city bus with their $7,000 in hand.

I was thirty years old, a mother of three, riding public transit, and living in an apartment in Central Phoenix. IRS letters and audits started because I hadn't paid taxes on my 1099 income, and I made a mistake on claiming our son Andres on the year his mom was scheduled to claim him. We had a mountain of debt that wasn't being addressed, and we had court dates for both a credit card and an unresolved ticket with the city due to a classic car Andrew owned that wasn't properly stored back when we lived at the house we short sold.

I'd been fighting so hard to dig up and out to create a better life for us with stability, certainty, and financial security since my very first counseling appointment when I was twenty, and somehow, ten years later, I felt like I had gotten nowhere.

I told Andrew that I wanted to go to sleep and never wake up. I had no fight left in me. Unable to get what I wanted and needed in my partnership with him and unable to solve anything without him, I felt stuck. So, I did what any reasonable adult would do, and I escaped by consuming cheesy tortellini, a bottle of red wine, and Reese's Peanut Butter Cup ice cream almost nightly.

# Finding Hope

One night I went to sleep after successfully escaping all of my feelings, and as usual, the sugar from everything I had consumed woke me up at about two a.m. Even though I was still tired, I couldn't go back to sleep. The TV in our room had been left on, and on it was an infomercial with this guy Tony Robbins, who was teaching people how they could achieve everything they wanted in life by managing their state. Whatever that meant.

The commercial was filled with images and testimonials of him with athletes and world leaders saying that he was the real deal, followed by normal people like us who had been where we were and who turned their life around and were living lives that were in alignment with what I saw for *our* ideal life.

He described how to do it, and it seemed like something I could do. That anyone could do, really. The commercial gave me more hope than I'd felt in a long time. I called and bought the CDs with money we didn't have, and when the offer to also sign me up for the coaching program was made, I laughed when the salesperson said, "Can you really afford not to?" No, my friend. But I also really can't afford to either. No. Really. Another time, perhaps.

When the CDs came, I would go across the street to the park every morning to walk and listen. I would eventually make my way to running and just took in the CDs over and over where Tony would say things like, "The quality of your life is in direct proportion to the quality of your emotions. Your emotions are a result of what you focus on, and what you focus on is what you get. And where focus goes, energy flows."

I learned that our focus is directed by the questions we ask ourselves, so to improve my focus, I needed to ask better questions. The first question was what did I have currently that I could be grateful for? That was a mind-bending thought at the time.

I was so obsessed with what I didn't have and what wasn't working that I never stopped to think about what I did have, and the truth was, I had a lot to be grateful for.

I had a beautiful family with three amazing kids and a husband who supported me on my crazy decision to leave my family business. We had a spacious and bright, safe apartment with a swimming pool steps away. We had clothes to wear. We could pay our living expenses on Andrew's salary. I was born in the United States, which meant I had a lot more opportunities than had I been born in a different country. I had skills and abilities that I'd learned and developed. I had a computer and internet. I had my health. My husband had great benefits, being employed by the US government. I had access to transportation. I had a family that loved me.

When I started to change my focus, my energy really did start to flow toward what was working and could work. I started to see opportunities and perspectives that I was unable to see before.

A thought that occurred to me was that I knew that my dad and brother had not solved their LTCI needs yet with the receptionist they'd hired, and I was desperate for a steady paycheck. It had been a year since I left, and while I still didn't want to go back to working the way I had before, there might be more than just that option.

I proposed a win/win situation for us all by returning temporarily as a contractor and in a way that no one would know I was there. I would come in and work uninterrupted and ghostwrite everything from quotes to communications so that we both got the help that we needed.

With that guaranteed income on the way, we asked Andrew's parents if we could borrow $1,500 to fix the VW so we were able to get back to a place where we had reliable transportation.

The work situation was perfect for me. The receptionist they'd hired was able to continue managing administrative tasks, which meant that I now had someone I could delegate to. That gave me the space to develop the new LTCI portion of our website and create marketing and communication campaigns to start to increase the sales we'd lost since I left. I kept waiting for something to feel off or weird, but it never did. In fact, it felt right and good.

We were all so grateful to have each other, and after a few months, we mutually agreed to have me come back full time.

The year was 2011, and by that time, we were in our third location but had outgrown it as well. We moved to a Class A office condo my dad purchased, and shortly after, I made my first-ever fire and subsequent hire who was insurance licensed and had the perfect skills, experience, and professionalism to manage all LTCI phones calls, walk-ins, quoting, case management, and state-by-state product management for both physical and digital materials.

With her help, I was able to further develop marketing and sales strategies and not only revive sales but even break previous records. We had solid systems and processes in our department, and things were running like a well-oiled machine.

This was my very first experience with the power of a team with the right people on it, who had proper training that I could delegate work to. What I learned was that even though there is a cost to having a new employee, that is only one side of the equation. Had I known how to articulate the value of what we would be able to produce if I had help, I could have justified the expense. We were both working in our strengths, and we were able to deliver outstanding results.

At home, things were starting to improve somewhat. I was able to pay bills on time, and we were able to save up enough money to buy the house across the street from Andrew's parents. With them in their sixties and seventies, we wanted to be close by for their potential future care. Our credit was still in the tank, but I was chipping away at it.

We received a phone call one afternoon from my mother-in-law, Hilda, who called to tell us that Ernie, my father-in-law, was having a heart attack.

He was hospitalized, and each day after dropping the kids off at school, I would go to his hospital room to work. With my medical underwriting background, I knew a lot of terminology, risks, complications, etc. and wanted to be an advocate for his care. Never knowing when a doctor might come in, someone needed to be there around the clock to ensure we didn't miss a single update.

After seven days in the hospital, he finally came home. We celebrated by having dinner together as a family. We were fortunate to have that moment with him that night because the next morning, he passed away at home.

The date was August 17, 2011.

My mother-in-law, Hilda, was hospitalized on the spot from the trauma, and Andrew and I needed to pull it together to figure out what to do next.

Planning a funeral is almost exactly the same as planning a wedding, except you're devastated, exhausted, and heartbroken, and instead of having months to plan, you have twenty-four hours.

His service was a perfect tribute to his amazing life, and almost as soon as it was over, the real work began. Hilda paid all of the bills and managed the checkbook, but Ernie managed everything else.

He had properties, vehicles, and investment accounts but no will, estate plan, or financial planner.

Wanting to help and thinking I should be able to "do it all," I inserted myself as the solution. I also started taking over Hilda's healthcare since her hospitalization, which I was happy to do.

Two weeks after Ernie passed away, I learned I was pregnant. I'd also been gaining weight really fast, and my starting weight in this pregnancy was 230 lbs.

I can remember listening to the stats about the players during football season and feeling humiliated that I weighed as much as a giant professional football player with my short 5'3" frame. I just didn't have it in me to address it at the time.

During my pregnancy I started having flashes in my left eye. I went straight to the doctor and learned that I now had a detached retina in that eye. The doctor that I really liked had moved out of state, and I was assigned a new doctor.

Just like the right eye in my pregnancy with Sophie, the left eye detached twice, and again my lens would need to be touched and a scleral buckle installed. He also said we would be installing an oil bubble instead of a gas bubble. I didn't ask questions but wish now that I had, because there is a residual oil bubble in my eyeball forever. When I asked him about it, he knew that would be the outcome and said I'd get used to it. Nice.

Unlike my right eye, I did not recover all of my vision in the left. I have a blind spot, poor vision that cannot be corrected through glasses/contacts, and poor peripheral vision. For what I can see, I have the pleasure of looking through an annoying oil bubble.

Somewhere between surgeries, I was interviewing a second staff member for my team because we needed the help and to prepare for my maternity leave. This time I insisted on taking off a full eight weeks, and I was committed to fully unplugging, having regretted the time I didn't take with Sophie.

Our little Liam Marshal Tautimes was born on May 4, 2012.

During my maternity leave, I spent time with my baby, had a cataract surgery, and experienced my first ever clarity break.

## My Industry Changes

Being unplugged from daily calls, emails, and meetings allowed me to just be still and think.

A lot had been going on in the LTCI industry even before I'd returned to the business, with companies exiting the marketplace, constant rate increase announcements, and a feeling of overall long-term market uncertainty.

It was becoming increasingly difficult to place business, and it was a constant mission to provide guidance and assurances to our downline about a future we didn't know anything more about than anyone else.

What I realized was that we needed to eliminate LTCI from our portfolio and focus exclusively on Medicare products. My brother and dad were successfully surpassing LTCI revenues with Medicare, and making this shift was a viable option.

Of course, this meant that I was putting the three of us in the LTCI department out of work, but it was clearly the best move for the company.

What I proposed was that our team move over to support Medicare. They would support brokers and the work my brother was doing, and I would shift my focus to working more *on* the business by building the proper infrastructure by building teams and culture, improving and streamlining processes, enhancing marketing and communications, and developing technology.

In three years, we went from seven to twenty-five people. In that time, we moved from a punch card time-management system to

Paychex and created our first 401(k). We created a structure for our broker service department, transitioned from an MS Access database to Salesforce, and moved event management from a manual process to digital registrations, eliminating hundreds of phone calls and emails. We built a lead distribution system with algorithms to reward behaviors. We developed a commission payment system, taking us from manual individual transactions to thousands of batched transactions. We developed a new contracting and hierarchy management system. We improved communications from health plans to brokers, becoming the timely and trusted source for news and information. We developed a new website that became the most valuable tool in our agent's toolboxes. We created an event called WAPCon that streamlined sixty days of work into two. We rebranded, moved offices again to accommodate our growing team, and attempted to build an Affordable Care Act company within WAP. That last one was an epic failure, but some of my best lessons came from that experience.

We had an incredible team, and whatever we could imagine together, we created.

Aside from removing obstacles, improving workflow, and making it easier for our agents and agencies to do business with us and us with them, my other primary focus at that time was our company culture. We were growing fast without any kind of policies and procedures, which meant that each day was like the Wild West. I didn't want to lose anyone in the chaos of it all.

100 percent of the time, whether it was culture, technology, managing people, or sharing my vision for the future, I was working in areas I had zero experience in and no guarantee we could deliver, but we had to try. I had to try. It was wildly imperfect, extremely stressful, and exhilarating all at the same time.

# Adjusting to a New Reality

Adjusting to our new world without my father-in-law was hard. Andrew and I proposed to Hilda and his sister Missi shortly after Ernie died that we would move in with his mom across the street to look after her, and his sister could live in our house.

I loved being there with Hilda, and I was closer to be able to help with settling the estate, meeting with her and her financial planner, and managing her doctors' appointments and medications. When we suggested living with her, I imagined her and me just sitting on the couch in the mornings together, sipping our coffee and chatting it up before I headed off to work for the day. That was a fantasy.

Instead of enjoying coffee with Hilda, my first sip was always at the same time, at the same place: on the freeway in my minivan, after my first deep inhale and exhale of the day—about ten minutes into my morning commute.

Every morning was a mad dash to get myself and the little ones ready, get them dropped off, conduct a full-court press at work for eight to ten hours straight where I almost never took breaks, always ate lunch at my desk, and rarely socialized. I would work up until the last minute, then race to get the baby and Sophie from after-school care and come home to Hilda and Andrew, who would be waiting for me while watching TV.

Most nights it was the same question: "Mari T, what are we doing for dinner?" To come home to two adults who were equally capable of helping with this detail was … frustrating.

In my world, there was no "FriYAY!" either. Weekends were just as hard, if not harder. At work, I could control my environment and predict my schedule. I could even close my door and put things on "Do Not Disturb." At home, I couldn't even go to the bathroom by myself.

Saturdays would begin with an early start on the laundry. Washing for six each week took the full weekend to accomplish. Once that was started, I'd drop off the dry cleaning, go to Costco and then the grocery store, because you just can't buy green onions at Costco. I used a meal-planning app called Paprika and did my best to meal plan and prep. I would bring everything home, wash it, and put it away. I would then do whatever other things needed to be done, like car washes, oil changes, tire rotations, yard work, or deep-dive cleaning on a certain area of the house. By the time Sunday came, I needed a day off, but instead of a day off, I headed into a new work week.

I was taking care of Hilda's finances and medical care and settling the estate, but I was still not addressing our finances or taxes. It was impossible to get to it all.

Around that time I was introduced to the book *Lean In*, written by Sheryl Sandberg, COO of Facebook. Reading her book was the first example of a female executive that I'd heard talking about what it was like to try to be and do it all. As I read, what I learned was that she wasn't trying to be and do it all, and it felt for the first time like I had permission to *not* feel like I needed to do everything, and that I wasn't unreasonable for asking for help.

What Sheryl taught me was that I needed to get to fifty-fifty partnership at home, or I wouldn't ever get to where I thought I could go in my career. I didn't know how I was going to do that, since I'd already tried to ask for help, but even just seeing that it was OK was helpful. I didn't take action right away, but I did have a new understanding planted in my head of what was possible.

Pressing on and not having made any changes, I struggled. I hadn't lost any baby weight after having Liam and was around 260 lbs. Work was more demanding than ever, and at home there was no opportunity for rest, peace, or space.

Arriving at the office one morning, I felt like I couldn't take one more step forward. I pulled into my parking space and just sat there. I had so much to do, I didn't even know where I was going to start, and I knew at the end of the day, I would still have more to do than I could ever manage. I started to break down. I had nothing left. Again.

I called Andrew to let him know that I was checking myself into the hospital, and I just wanted him and everyone to leave me alone. I would have checked into a hotel to just sleep, eat, and watch TV, but no one would have understood that. At least if I was at the hospital, I could get some rest and relief for a day, maybe.

He asked me not to go in and met me in the parking lot of the hospital. He asked me what was going on, and I shared with him that I needed help. I needed his help settling his dad's estate. I needed help with dinner. I needed more flexibility to work. I needed to have some space. I needed him to help maintain the vehicles. I needed him to help with our finances. I needed him to sit with me each week and plan and prepare for the week. I needed his help with the kids in the mornings. I needed him to take the dry cleaning. I needed him to help with chores.

He promised to start helping, asked me not to check myself in, and I didn't.

Time passed. I kept doing everything (50 percent of the problem), and he kept not doing anything (50 percent of the problem), and nothing changed.

Hilda then started to have some health issues that caused her to fall and become forgetful. Because I had the "flexible" job compared to my husband and sister-in-law, who had government jobs, and because I managed her care, I said I would work from home and look after her.

I decided that while I was home, I would dig into our mail that had been piling up for over two months that I just couldn't or wouldn't get to.

A letter from Sophie's school was in the stack, and when I opened it, I learned we had a preset appointment with the headmaster. She had been late to school too many times in that quarter, and it was time for a conversation. I was so embarrassed that I immediately started to cry.

I called Andrew to let him know. His response to me was, "What kind of a mom doesn't get her kid to school on time?" He laughed at me. I hung up.

When he got home that night from work, I tried to talk with him about it. He wouldn't talk to me, so I had to follow him around the house to talk *at* him and eventually ended up in the garage.

I told him that I needed help in the mornings to get the kids off to school, and maybe instead of hitting the snooze button and just worrying about himself each morning, he could help me get the kids ready too.

"Oh, so it's *my* fault that you can't get Sophie to school on time. You're ridiculous."

That was *it*. I was so furious that I felt like I was going to black out. I went into our room with a handful of trash bags, and I began to empty my drawers into the bags. The only things I needed to take with me were the things I needed to maintain a professional image, so the world didn't know my life was falling apart at home.

As I carried my bags out the door of my bedroom, my sister-in-law came and walked me back in. She closed the door behind her and gave me a look I'd never seen before, and it was clearly reflecting the *crazy* on my face.

# The Road to Recovery

She talked me off the ledge. The only thing that stopped me from walking out the door that day was the thought of my baby girl and the heartache on her little four-year-old face watching me leave.

I went to my car and sat in the driver's seat. I wasn't going to leave. I just needed space to clear my head and think. In my car was the only place I ever seemed to have any peace and quiet.

What came up was that my life didn't look anything like what I thought it should. My thirty-third birthday was around the corner, which gave me a little more than two years until I was going to be turning thirty-five. I had two years to make sure that thirty-five wasn't going to be a repeat of thirty, meaning a total miss on where I thought I should be compared to where I actually was.

I had *plenty* of runway to make massive changes, and with my anger, I had all the leverage I needed to do it.

Where I started was thinking about who I was before I became what everyone else needed me to be. What came up for me was the memory of the loss of my brother and how I used to be so driven, with a sense of urgency to want to live as much as I possibly could knowing that I could be gone tomorrow.

> There was no way I was going to die in a life that was 100% about serving everyone else.

That then made me think: if I died tomorrow, would I be proud of who I was at this exact moment? Would I really be able to say that I had done everything I could with my life?

When I had that thought, I immediately thought that there was *no way* I was going to die in a life that was 100 percent about serving everyone else, never having traveled anywhere or having experienced anything and buried under a mound of debt, tax issues, and fat.

I was no longer going to live for everyone else. I was going to spend my time focusing on my health, my kids, and my career, in that order. My health had to come first because without it, I wasn't the best mom I could be for my kids.

At that moment on that day, I joined Weight Watchers. I downloaded the C25K (Couch to 5K) app, and I wrote out what I wanted. The next day I set an appointment with a naturopathic doctor.

I started to feel better, look better, and do better. I was starting to recover myself.

Russell Brand says in his book *Recovery: Freedom from Our Addictions* that he believes each of us is like a seed. A seed has everything that it needs to grow big, tall, and strong. Sometimes, though, seeds are planted in sand or surrounded by barbed wire or other adverse conditions. That doesn't, however, change the initial capacity of that seed to become something great; it just needs to be replanted into a better environment, and then it will grow to the full potential it always had the capacity to have.

Recovery and/or self-improvement isn't about creating ourselves or turning ourselves into something we're not. It is about recovering who we always had the potential to be.

Part of taking better care of myself also meant protecting my time better, and to do that, I created a list of things I was going to *stop* doing, which was as important as the things that I wanted to start doing.

I was beginning to heal from the inside out. The trust and integrity that I started to build with myself when I consistently did what I said I was going to do gave me even more energy, fuel, and capacity.

In our business, we started getting noticed on a national level because of our growth. For the first time, Paul and I were called to fly to an event hosted by Cigna in Miami, Florida. I was down 20 lbs. to 240 and was actually feeling pretty good about myself. I felt strong, beautiful, and like I was taking charge of my life.

On that trip, walking on the sandy beach and playing in the warm Atlantic Ocean, surrounded by families and lovers on vacation, I became even more inspired about what was possible in life.

I shared this vision with Andrew when I returned home. He would agree that traveling and exploring would be cool, but as soon as I brought it up, the fantasy was gone. It was never going to happen. We never talked about or planned how we would free ourselves from our debt issues so that we could do things like this together. We would also never sit down with a calendar and plan anything. When I tried, he didn't see the value in it. It would turn into an argument, and so I stopped trying to plan together with him and just continued to live by my own planner.

Other families would ask, "What are you doing for [insert spring break, fall break, winter break, summer, holiday]?" for polite conversation, and the answer was perpetually *nothing*. Because that takes money and planning. And we had and did neither.

I shared with him that it felt to me like his mission was to get home, to stay home, and to figure out more things that we could do at home while working on the home.

I couldn't be more opposite. I felt like life was all happening *out there* and that home was a base. It's where we sleep, eat, and restore before going back out into the world to experience and do more things.

Without a shared vision about creating our best life as a family, with values that were out of alignment, and a partnership that didn't feel like partnership at all, it was clear to me that we had nothing left and that try as I might, I did not have the power to change him or our situation for the better.

# The Hardest Words I've Ever Had to Say

On April 14, 2015, I finally got up the nerve to tell Andrew that I wanted a divorce. I spent the rest of that day and night telling him why. About all the times I felt left alone to manage every difficult detail of our life. How it was impossible to improve our situation alone, but it was equally impossible to get him to engage, and about all the times I'd tried and asked.

He asked me why I didn't yell more, why I didn't say more along the way. I told him that my punishment for ever pushing back or calling anything out was a guaranteed three days of silent treatment with no resolution or discussion at the end of it, so it was pointless. I'd been successfully trained to keep it all inside and to just keep taking it and keep moving forward.

I moved out in May. We watched our boys graduate from high school while living in different homes and sitting apart at graduation. I felt so proud of them and so devastated to not be celebrating them as a family. They deserved so much more.

# I Begin as Co-CEO, and the Transformation Begins: Four Days with Tony Robbins' Business Mastery

That same year, my dad had announced that he was going to be stepping down as CEO. Paul was in charge of finance, sales, industry relationships with agents, agencies, and carriers, and I was in charge of operations, marketing, technology, teams, culture, and relationships outside of our industry, where I spent time trying to learn how other people were innovating in their respective industries.

When my dad announced he was stepping down, I felt like Paul and I were equally unqualified to take the seat. That's right: I said "unqualified" because I was certain that neither of us had the skills to take the company to the next level as we were, but we could certainly learn, and that's, of course, an advantage of being in a small, family-owned entrepreneurial company. I approached my dad with examples of other companies that had successful co-CEO models and shared that I thought it would be perfect because our skill sets were so complimentary.

In January of 2016, we announced that Paul and I were partnering as co-CEO's. As twins, it also made for a really great story.

I shared with my dad that I would be spending the next two years working to help get us qualified. Speaking for myself, I said that if I couldn't get us to where I thought we should be, I would step down from the position.

I started to research the fastest way to get us business training and learned that Tony Robbins offered a program called Business Mastery. I didn't know it back when I purchased his CDs, but Tony Robbins owned thirty-plus companies and understood the art and science of business, and also maintained an incredible network of trainers and teachers that he pulled together to help educate the rest of us entrepreneurs.

It was a five-day long course that promised to deliver $1 million in value or more to our business on the first day. Considering the ticket was $10K per person for the cheap seats, that was a pretty solid guarantee. We traveled to West Palm Beach, Florida, in January 2016 to attend what would be for me the most transformational events of my entire life and career.

We learned *so many* amazing things that were new concepts. Things like:

- The number one chokehold in your business is *you*. Your business can only get better when *you* get better. He teaches that 80 percent of success in business is related to psychology, and 20 percent is about skill, knowledge, and talent.

- There are three types of business leaders, and while we all have all three types inside of us, we typically have a single more dominant quality. The three types are:

  - Artist: without this person, the business does not exist. They are the craft of the business and are consistently honing it.

  - Manager: this person brings everything down to the ground, holds people accountable, and gets things done.

  - Entrepreneur: Risk-taker, sees the possibilities, and pushes the company into the future.

We learned that Paul was the artist. My brother was a brilliant subject-matter expert, and he was the heart and soul of the development of our downline as well as carrier partnerships. Without what he was able to do on the business development and relationship side, we had nothing.

Prior to Paul really owning that, my dad did, and he also was comfortable taking risks, and he was an OK manager too. None of us were really *great* managers … we knew how to work hard, knew what needed to be done, let each other fail and learn and just GSD'd. Our form of management was to hire people that could be thrown into the deep end just like us and figure out a way to swim.

What I learned was that I was an entrepreneur. I didn't see myself that way and felt a little jarred by the revelation. After some thought, though, I realized that I was consistently pushing us to the next evolution in our business, whether it be technology, deciding to shut something down, deciding to start something up, to hire and build teams, to drive culture, and to have a vision for the future.

- Every business is in a stage of life from infancy to death, and there are characteristics that define each stage. In the middle of that, there is a zone of maximization, and that's where we want to get to and stay (and he, of course, teaches us how to do that).

- Inbound marketing lessons from David Meerman Scott— connecting with our audiences by informing and educating, not interrupting and disrupting. Also lessons in Newsjacking and other marketing tips.

- Business finance lessons from Keith Cunningham (the Rich Dad in Robert Kiyosaki's book *Rich Dad, Poor Dad*), who taught us how to read balance sheets and profit and loss statements but that ultimately that doesn't teach us where to dig for gold in our business. He taught us how to figure that out much earlier so that we were focused on the right activities much earlier in the game to influence the scoreboards of our business.

- Maximization lessons from Jay Abraham, learning how to increase revenue by creating more opportunities within what you have instead of the far more expensive cost of acquisition, but without changing your core focus.

- 7 Forces of Business Mastery: we learned the seven forces and how to stay laser-focused on them and how to reach the ultimate objective of creating a raving fan culture.

There were more speakers and lessons than just this lineup, but these were my favorites.

Each day ranged from ten–fourteen hours per day, and we averaged over 20K steps *at our seats* with no scheduled breaks or food provided.

*I loved it.* The uncertainty in how the day was going to go had my brain and my body awake in a way that I'd never quite experienced before.

Part of the reason there is no set time agenda, too, is because Tony takes as long as it takes. These events are objective driven, not agenda driven. If he's working with a business owner on their problem, he goes all the way in, whether it's a twenty-minute conversation or a two-hour conversation. He doesn't quit until that person's issues are solved, and when he worked with that person, we *all* learned from the example.

Above all else, there was one lesson that Tony wanted to make sure we walked away knowing. Considering how he sets it up, I would venture to say that it is the most important lesson of the entire event.

On the first day, he asked us to get into teams of eight, to pick a team leader, a team name, brand, and chant. Our objective over the duration of the conference was to figure out how to provide more value to the room than any of the other teams. There would be two teams on stage at the end of the event: the learning team and the winning team.

We gathered into a team, and someone asked who wanted to be our team leader. With the new knowledge I had that I was officially an entrepreneur and risk-taker, I decided to start living into it on purpose. I raised my hand. My dad and brother looked at me in a sort of, "Oh my God, Mari, put your hand down" kind of way ... and the other new people didn't know me. I would venture to guess that because I was a female and clocking in at about two hundred pounds, there were some underlying biases that I was painfully aware of and even had about myself, but I kept my hand raised. It was like some force inside of me that I'd never tapped into before. As soon as the team agreed to let me lead, I felt like Ron Burgundy in *Anchorman* after he jumps into the bear pit to save Veronica Corningstone when he says, "I *immediately* regret this decision!" That's how I felt inside, but I didn't show it on the outside.

For the rest of that day and the next two days, I led my team in a group obsession over how we could provide more value to our customer (the room) than any other team. Somehow, we were able to continue to learn while simultaneously obsessing over various strategies for providing value.

I'd never worked so hard to come up with an idea before. Ideas always just came to me whenever and wherever, but I never had to actually produce one on a tight timeline before. I was afraid that maybe I'd been lucky with my ideas up until then, but if asked to really produce something on purpose and on time, maybe I wasn't capable of that.

It was so frustrating. It was like trying to start a fire with anything we could find. From time to time, we would get sparks, but we couldn't fan it into a flame.

By the morning of the fourth day, I pitched an idea to my team. They seemed to feel sorry for me. One of them looked over and said, "It's OK, Mari, we're not going to get it. We did everything we could."

I started to sit down and settle into the reality that we weren't going to win, and I also took comfort in the fact that my team was OK with it and was letting me off the hook. I sat there and pictured us not doing anything else for the remaining day and just quitting. I pictured how I would feel walking through the airport on the way home. I pictured how I would feel when I got home, knowing I'd given up. This was about my own integrity with myself, no one else. And when would I ever have an opportunity like this again anyway? What did I have to lose?

Giving up did not work for me. With or without my team, I was going to keep going. There was still time.

On the first day of the event, I'd created a Twitter profile for our team, and we were tweeting along the way. Our content was being liked and shared by Business Mastery, which meant that they could see us.

That thought mixed in with what we'd just learned from David Meerman Scott about newsjacking (a way to leverage other stories and make them your own).

I had it. I knew what we needed to do.

If we could capture and promote what all of the other teams were doing on Twitter to Business Mastery, we would be providing value to the room because we would be helping the teams by giving them greater visibility to Business Mastery, and it would be helping Business Mastery assess what all of the teams were doing at a glance on our Twitter feed.

I told my team, and immediately the spark caught fire. Tony said there were 1,500 people in the room, assuming those were all attendees. That meant that there were about 187 team stories to capture. We needed to get to work.

The coolest thing started to happen as we took this approach. We were able to get outside our team self-obsession and started actually seeing everyone else.

People had created fundraisers for Tony's charities through photo booths. Others were raising funds to send military veterans to Tony's Unleash the Power Within (UPW) event. *Way* cool. Others were providing Emergen-C packets to the room, and others were providing snacks. There were websites launched, parties thrown, and flyers for things everywhere! It was amazing to see how much innovation happened inside of three days, and all while we were equally focused on learning from world-class speakers.

> We were able to get outside our team self-obsession and started actually seeing everyone else.

During a break, I went to our hotel and used their printer in the business center to print out simple black-and-white flyers that said, "Caring Is Sharing—We've Shared What *Your* Team Is Doing with Business Mastery," and then posted our Twitter handle. I purposely changed the order of the words from "Sharing Is Caring" to get them to pause for a moment longer to look at it, assuming it would irritate them like it irritated me.

We put the flyers in the one place every single attendee of the event was sure to go—bathroom stalls and mirrors.

Once I knew we had a solid idea and were executing on it, it was so fun and relaxing to be able to explore what everyone was doing and to get to acknowledge them for their efforts. I could also relax knowing that at a minimum, we'd done everything we could and didn't give up.

At two a.m. in a hotel lobby, several of us were huddled around a table with all of the flyers we'd collected from various teams. At one point, a young woman came dancing in through the sliding doors and, with a huge smile on her face, made her way over to our table. She asked why we didn't go to the party that night hosted by a different team.

I shared with her our campaign and what we were up to and asked if she was interested in telling us what her team was doing and if she wanted us to share.

She was thrilled. She said her team's name was Team Impact, and she described their efforts. They were doing several things, each of them truly meaningful and impressive. And she was like a bright light herself, too, which I just loved. I told her that we would share their story and wished her luck.

The next day was the final day, and I had a new idea. I was going to finish posting the rest of the stories, and then I was going to recommend that Team Impact win the award. They were perfectly branded; they did the most good for the room that I'd seen, and their energy was amazing.

I had just finished the final post when the young lady from Team Impact that we met at the hotel came running up to me with her team leader and said, "This is the lady I was telling you about that is going to share with Business Mastery what we're doing!"

I shared with him that I'd seen what many of the teams had done, and that I would be promoting them as our chosen winner for the event to Business Mastery.

They thanked me and asked me if I wanted to join their team. They'd been asking other people, but most had declined. *Of course* I wanted to join the winning team!

They brought my team and me a handful of branded neon shirts. I handed the shirts to my teammates, asked them to put them on, and told them that we were joining Team Impact.

I was uncharacteristically sure of myself on this and even a little forceful. I said it with such conviction and enthusiasm that the moment of hesitation expressed on their faces was immediately replaced with a smile and willingness to just go with it.

Everything inside of me at this point was certain that we were going to be on stage with Tony Robbins. So much so that I ran to the bathroom to tighten the slack in my bra straps.

At "Tony" events there is a *lot* of jumping around, which I fully participated in. Jumping around as a large woman requires a world-class utilitarian sports bra which I did not own, and I was *not* going to get on stage with Tony Robbins in a neon T-shirt made for a small 9-year-old boy without proper support.

When I got back from the bathroom minutes later, Team Impact came to get us and invited us into their section, which was at the very front of the room, right in front of the stage where Tony was.

Everything started to move in slow motion for me. I was watching my team celebrating and dancing. I was standing back and observing the connections and comradery we'd created in such a short time with the deposits we'd made in other teams. I was watching Tony onstage feet away from me. I got what I came for. I got my $1 million in value. I learned that I was a leader who had vision, tenacity, and skills to lead a team to victory.

Tony first announced the learning team, and even though I was pretty sure it wasn't us, I still braced myself just in case. It wasn't. I breathed a sigh of relief. After a discussion with them about what didn't work, he transitioned to announcing the winning team.

He described the things they had done to provide more value to the room than anyone else. He then called Team Impact to the stage. That in itself was such a winning moment, that I had personally predicted the winning team just like Tony. To me it meant that I had even more leadership skills and abilities than I knew I had coming into this event.

I was *so* happy for them and watched them dance/run their way to the stage. As soon as they got up there, Tony was about to continue, but the leader stopped the show. Tony started talking with him about something, and the next thing I knew, Tony was looking at me and my team. He then said, "OK," and waved us up to the stage.

Tony talked with the winning team as we stood behind them like flies on a wall, and we listened to Tony interview them about their decisions and lessons on success.

At the end, as we proceeded off the stage, I stopped in front of Tony. I'd made it this far; why not go this last small step to hug this man that I appreciated so much who, for a second time, helped me change my life? I hugged him. He hugged me back.

On that day, I knew with certainty that I was a leader. I didn't have to have a certificate. I didn't have to be a man. I didn't have to have the agreement of people around me. I didn't have to be in perfect health. I could lead starting right from where I was in that moment and on that day.

## 1 . 4

# Living on Purpose

Business Mastery moved me from a place of unconscious incompetence (being unaware of my skill and lack of proficiency) in business to conscious incompetence (aware of the skill but not yet proficient).

Conscious incompetence is my absolute least favorite place to be, especially as I get older. The more experience I gain, the more proficient I have become in various skills. And I quite like the perks that come with proficiency.

Perks like:

1. The significance I get to experience because I'm the "go-to" person.

2. The comfort of knowing the path ahead.

3. The ease with which I can get something done.

4. The pride I feel when I do something well over and over again.

5. The peace of mind knowing that I'm on the right track for bigger future opportunities.

6. The ability to innovate with confidence and change what hasn't worked in the past.

The perks are actually emotions and feelings that I get to experience on a regular basis. Feelings of comfort, peace, ease, pride, and significance.

Since feelings and emotions are a direct result of our thoughts, when I think of something like the deal I just closed, the words of affirmation I received two months ago, the idea I shared that became the way we do business, and so on, I get to feel all of those great feelings. And I might often think back to these things whenever I need a dose of good *feels*.

On the contrary, when I try new things I instead feel like I'm dumb because I don't know how. Or I can't see the path ahead and am filled with uncertainty. Or that everything is harder, and I have to fire up my brain and body each and every time to do the thing, and even then, I don't do it well. Or maybe embarrassed because I can't do it right, but I feel like I should be able to, because look at this laundry list of other things I *can* do right. Or I'm unsure if I'll ever be good enough at this to level up. Or that my ideas don't mean much because I don't have enough experience yet.

All of my stress chemicals come out to play instead of euphoric chemicals and make me want to get defensive, cry, or leave the situation. All the signals my body gives me say that this isn't where I need to be or what I need to be doing.

This becomes increasingly true as I get older. Maybe it does for you too.

While learning new things and realizing how much we don't know is extremely uncomfortable, what is even more uncomfortable is the thought that I might face my deathbed someday never knowing what I could have actually done.

If we're going to learn, grow, and achieve everything we can see in our mind's eye for our lives and the lives of those we love and influence, we're going to have to get comfortable with conscious incompetence. We are going to have to consistently embrace the *suck*.

See this diagram for the four stages of competency.

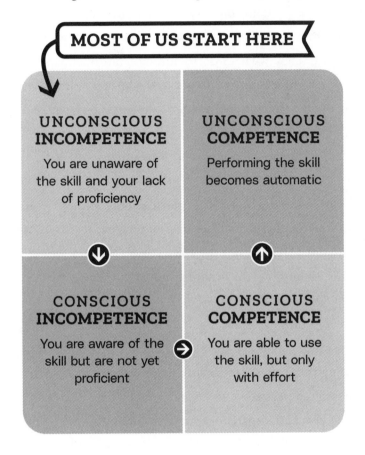

## Learning at Warp Speed

Since the kids were with Andrew half of the time, I was able to fully immerse myself in working on my health and my personal and professional growth, because if I'd learned anything at Business Mastery, it was that nothing was going to get better until I got better.

In 2015 and 2016, I read twenty books and listened to hundreds of hours of podcasts, from *How I Built This* to *TED Radio Hour*, from *Freakonomics Radio* to Tony's. I felt like I couldn't learn enough fast enough. Every available minute was spent learning, listening, reading and growing.

Around the same time, my dad elevated two of our employees to help advise Paul and me and balance out our leadership. It was a brilliant move on his part. We went from the three of us kind of thinking we knew what to do to adding team members with more education and experience. With our newly formed team, we had sales, finance, operations, and marketing represented at the table.

We started to build even better infrastructure, teams, and culture, but it didn't happen overnight, and it was pretty rough for what felt like forever.

To make it more bearable, I prioritized our culture because what kept me up at night was the fact that I knew that *they* knew we didn't have our shit together, and my theory was that they would hang in there with us longer if they could at least feel that we cared for them, which of course we did.

I would promise them regularly a future where we had policies and procedures, a vision for exactly where we were going and how we were going to get there, and assure them that just around the corner, we'd have all the answers.

I was always transparent about what I didn't know and what I was trying to learn, because I have no poker face, and I knew delivering anything other than the truth wouldn't end well.

My brother *did* know what he was delivering and where things were going regarding our products and services, so we all rested in the comfort that at least we'd be able to keep revenue coming in while we sorted out some of our operational issues.

Despite most days feeling like we weren't doing things perfectly, we were experiencing a lot of wins. We had the right people on the bus, and they were in the right seats. We knew exactly what our product offering was and the best way to deliver it. We were consistently creating industry-leading technology. We developed an industry-leading conference. And the biggest win was that we were able to get really good at creating raving fans with our team so they could help us create raving fans of our clients.

It was dreamy by all entrepreneurial accounts, but it wasn't all unicorns and rainbows, and in every next book that I read, I was hoping for some kind of revelation about the very best way for us to structure the company, the book that would help me learn how to be a better manager, the tips on exactly how often we should meet and what we should be talking about exactly, and *who* should be in those meetings.

These seemed like such simple issues that should have obvious answers, but we just didn't know. Sure, we were having meetings and managing people, but I knew it could *clearly* be done better.

Everyone was working insane hours. Everyone was doing their best with their areas, and I distinctly remember telling them to take ownership of whatever their thing was and that someday, when we'd look back on these days, they would have had a hand in shaping the Western Asset Protection way. I knew that everyone doing things their own way wasn't scalable, but the point was that at least *someone* was setting a standard for now, and we'd pull it all together eventually, when we had more time.

One of the biggest challenges we would encounter in our new leadership roles would be facing the loss of an account that represented $1.2 million in revenue.

We spent countless hours as a leadership team working to figure out the best path forward. After cutting as many costs as we could, we still needed to let eleven employees go. Paul would manage the difficult task of calling all of the external partners and managing the relationship blows there, and my job was to let eleven of our twenty-five employees go.

It was the single most difficult day of my career, which I am certain paled in comparison to how they felt.

Nothing will ever feel right about making decisions like this. I would walk laps and laps around the building, processing if there was any other way. Agonizing over which positions we'd picked and why. When *every* person is the right person on the bus, what do you do? When you have a personal connection and relationship with each person on the team, how do you decide? What will it do to their families and their relationships? What will come of the employees that stay?

Leadership is hard. It requires us to dig deep and at times to put the needs of the business before the needs of the very people you have grown to love. I say "at times" because our people came first 98 percent of the time. But it's also about knowing that 2 percent of the time, we had to put the business before our people; otherwise there wouldn't be a business.

When faced with something this difficult, some questions to ask ourselves are things like: What can I do to help this person the most with their next move? What can the company contribute to their transition (severance, technology, job placement support, etc.)? How can this announcement and process be done in a way that generates maximum dignity for this person?

I don't know that we did all the right things, but we did the best we knew how at the time, and I've since learned things I could have done better.

# Home vs. Work: Facing the Reality

The excruciating and at times exhilarating days at work and all the lessons learned did not translate back into home life. In the business, I felt accomplished, relevant, important, and often in control of my time.

At home, I rarely felt accomplished or in control. And unlike work, roles weren't clearly defined or discussed, they were assumed. I just assumed the roles that Andrew's parents had assumed, his mother being a stay-at-home mom and his dad being a provider, which meant that I did all the things that his mother did because I wanted to be loved by him. I should add, too, that because his dad was a federal marshal and traveled much of the time, she did 100 percent of everything related to managing the home, vehicles, kids, meals, yardwork, housekeeping, and bill paying. So, I too did all of that. He didn't ask, I just did.

Another challenging aspect of home life is that no one (of course) asks to schedule a meeting with you when they want to discuss or share something with you. Kids share what they want/need to share when they want/need to share it. And I think that is beautiful … and what it means is that we must be present "on demand." Our spouses/partners, too, are more "on demand" at home as well, because when else are they going to talk with you about their day, their stresses, their wins, and household things?

There was a study that I'd heard on NPR once that tracked working moms in their work environments and then in their homes in the evening. Their cortisol (stress hormone) was being measured throughout the day, and what they were trying to determine was whether home life or work life was more stressful. The study found that home life was more stressful.

It had to do with a feeling of being in control and I later learned from Tony Robbins that 100 percent of the time that we experience stress in our life, it's because we are focused on or experiencing something that is out of our control. I've examined when I feel the most stressed and have found it's true - I wanted to be in control of something I didn't have control of.

The former CEO of PepsiCo, Indra Nooyi, said on the Freakonomics podcast (ep. 316) "these jobs give you crowns, and you can just leave those crowns in the garage. When you come home, don't try to pretend that you're still the big boss, because you're not."

> **I wanted to be in control of something that I didn't have control of.**

At home, your accomplishments mean little (unless they equate to more time off with them or more money to get the family what they need). You don't get to schedule meetings with your family once a week and ask them to just post their issues, dreams and thoughts in Slack or an email outside of the weekly family meeting. You must be present for them on demand. It's the right thing to do, but it can be challenging.

We need time and space in our head. Time to think. Time to be. As a mother of four kids, especially when the kids were young, time in my head was scarce. When everyone needed me to be "on" 100 percent of my waking hours in work and at home, there was no me. It's how I lost myself in the first place.

# Facing a Brave New World—Alone

Having left my marriage, diving 100 percent into my work and leadership role every waking moment that I didn't have the kids, I had space and time to learn and think.

Thinking that all of my answers to where I was trying to go were just around the corner, I constantly sought more help, inspiration, and training.

In March of 2017, Paul and I decided we were ready for our next dose of Tony Robbins. We attended his UPW event, which is his introductory program. There, we signed up for a package deal to attend his Life Mastery, Wealth Mastery, and Date with Destiny events in October and December later that year.

When I returned from the event and looked through my list of outstanding tasks/to-dos, I was reinspired to keep checking things off that I wanted or needed to get done. Divorce was still on the list.

If there was a choice between a column of "wanted" and a column of "needed to get done," our divorce would have lived in the latter. It was never something that I wanted, but I really didn't see any other way, and we needed to get it done.

It had been two years since I moved out, and the first set of papers I filed expired. I didn't push it then, but the second set was approaching the expiration, and I needed to ask Andrew to move forward so we could both move on.

When I reached out and asked him, he shared with me that he hadn't signed the papers yet because he was hopeful that we would someday get back together.

I was extremely deliberate not to ever give him that hope. We maintained a friendship where we would do things together as a family when the kids had birthdays, holidays, or sporting events. But

I maintained a distance emotionally so that I never gave him the impression we would be getting back together.

I was so intentional about this that he would tell me that I was as cold as ice. He couldn't believe the switch I was able to turn off/on when it came to our life together and our love.

What he didn't know was that it was because I loved him so much that I acted that way. I never wanted to hurt him again, and I was certain that things would never change in his life to the degree that I would need for us to be together, and so I didn't ever want to give him false signals or hope. To me, that would be even more unkind than to be black and white about it.

Every once in a while, he would send me a text late at night, asking me if I was up. It was his way of reaching out. To bridge a conversation. To try to connect. I would see it, and I would delete it.

I would ignore my heart and my body and remind myself that this was just the way it had to be. It broke my heart to break his heart. I can only imagine how it felt for him to receive nothing in return.

He sent me a final email in an attempt to connect, and in this email, he sent me a song, and the email just said, "This isn't how our story ends."

The song he sent was "Jealous" by Labrinth.

> *And I told you when you left me*
> *There's nothing to forgive*
> *But I always thought you'd come back, tell me all you found was*
> *Heartbreak and misery*
> *It's hard for me to say, I'm jealous of the way*
> *You're happy without me*

This isn't how I *wanted* our story to end either.

I evaluated it again. I evaluated *us* again.

# A Life Together...

Go back to a life where there was no me? Where I couldn't grow as an executive? Where I couldn't travel the world and enjoy new experiences? Where I couldn't have friends and do things socially? Where I was surely going to regain my weight and be unhealthy again? Where I was going to have to live in someone else's home and life, setting aside my own life?

While I agreed with him, that this wasn't how our story should end, I knew that it had to. Because I wasn't willing to sacrifice my life anymore, and I knew that I never would again. Not for anyone. Which didn't mean I didn't love him or my kids or his family. It meant that I loved myself. And when I thought of what I wanted my kids to see an example of, it was an example of a life lived well, not a life of total sacrifice.

It wasn't easy, though, to stay focused. Every time we did something together for the kids' sake as a family, it was like a slice of the vision I'd seen where I was living my fulfilled life that also included him and ultimately us all together. It was so nice. And of course, I would sneak glances at his striking features, his beautiful black hair, his giant, muscular arms—the same arms that used to hold me tight and that used to make me feel warm and safe.

I would look at our beautiful children. Liam, who looked just like him, and Sophie, who looked just like me. I would think of our kids growing up in two different houses. It was excruciating. It was not what I wanted.

With only days left before the expiration of this second set of divorce papers, Andrew came to my house with the papers in hand.

Andrew is not a speech type of person. He isn't one to ever try to sell himself, or anything else, for that matter. He is confident, and he knows who he is. When he does go to say something to try to get a message across, it's a big deal. And it was clear that before he gave me the papers, he had something to say.

I could feel his nervousness. It felt like he'd probably rehearsed what he wanted to say on the way over. Maybe he did. Maybe he had been for months before that.

I listened to him with every cell in my body.

He shared with me that he did not want this divorce. If I felt that this was what I needed, he told me that he loved me so much that he would be willing to give it to me to let me go.

He said that this divorce was the best worst thing that ever happened to him, following it up by saying that he had learned so much.

He handed me the papers, which signified that he was at the end of what he wanted to say.

The brevity wasn't an indication of a lack of depth, passion, or emotion. It was the opposite.

I could feel every word, and my heart was powerfully connected to his in what would be one of the most profound moments in our lives together.

Even more powerful was that he had no intention to stay, to talk through anything. He had no outcome planned for this speech and delivery. He said what he felt, and he was going to leave.

I couldn't let him leave. I wanted him to stay.

I asked him, "What did you learn?"

The next thing I knew, we'd been sitting for some time, him talking and me listening.

As I listened, inside my head and my heart, all kinds of signals and feelings were firing off. The voice that had been protecting him and me was very present, saying, "Stay the course. We don't want anyone to hurt anymore." And then there was a new voice, "Yes, but isn't this what we needed to happen in order for this relationship to work? For him to show up as the person who learned all of these things that he's sharing?"

I couldn't trust *any* of the voices or feelings in my body, so I did what any person in their right mind would do in that moment, and I invited him to watch an episode of *Game of Thrones* with me.

He knew I was a fan, and he'd never seen it, so it was a fantastic excuse to just keep him in my house while I processed this new information, and in a way that didn't give him any confusing green lights. He'd stayed and watched things with us before, so it wasn't too inviting or confusing of a request.

We watched that episode, and then he went home. I invited him over for the second episode, which turned into the second season and then the third.

I was cautious. I was watching and feeling and waiting for something to not feel right, but no flags were ever raised. One night, I fell asleep. He tucked me in bed and left.

We both proceeded with caution as we continued to talk, reconnect, and test the waters with what this new relationship could look like.

If we were going to move forward, it would be 100 percent different this time. Meaning I would be different. I would show up braver and more courageous to say what I need and to fight for it much earlier. He agreed to show up differently too. Instead of me planning alone, *we* would plan and create our life together. *We* would travel and have adventures. *We* would learn and grow together. *We* would live in our own home that we love very close to family but not with family, unless it ever became physically necessary. *We* would manage our finances together and get healthy together.

With this newly defined relationship, we started to date again secretly. On our first date out, we didn't actually know what to do with ourselves, so we ended up walking around at The Container Store. We were really more like awkward teenagers without a plan. It was new. It was easy. It was exciting. It was right.

One night after a date, he sent me this text when he got home: "A woman cannot change a man. A man changes himself because he loves her."

We let our kids know we were dating again. Well, our adult kids had already figured it out, but we also shared it with the wee ones.

Soon Andrew was spending the night at the apartment, which Sophie and Liam loved until they didn't. They had a good thing going with two separate homes and our undivided attention. Now their attention from us was shared with each other, which was a difficult transition period, but I'm certain the love and safety they needed more was to see and feel us together.

> We stuck to our guns and continued to put our marriage first and then our kids.

We stuck to our guns and continued to put our marriage first and then our kids, because that's the healthy family they deserved—whether they knew it or not.

Paul and I still had our Date with Destiny event with Tony Robbins to attend in West Palm Beach, Florida. I really wanted Andrew to go because this event is powerful for relationships, and I couldn't see how we would be coming back together in ours and *not* attend this event together.

This was a really big first step for us, though, because part of the reason we don't fly anywhere is that Andrew has a deep anxiety around flying. We attended a class at the airport hosted by a former pilot, where he helped teach people how to overcome their fear of flying, and the next day we were on a plane to Florida. It would be the farthest we'd ever traveled together and was proof to me that he was willing to work on meeting me halfway in the life that we wanted to build together.

Andrew stepped up in all the ways that I needed, and very consistently. In fact, I felt like I was the one who needed to step up most of the time to keep up with him. If we had an argument, he was the mature one in the conversation, forcing me to level up. He was accountable, loving, and firm. This new version of him was nothing short of dreamy. He made me feel safe and secure and that he was the leader I always wanted and needed him to be.

He is also incredibly tuned in to my emotional needs and status and now knows how to be there for me without solving anything, which amazes me because I don't even know what I'm feeling half of the time.

I was riding the Peloton one evening, and a Red Hot Chili Peppers song came on, which was one of my brother David's favorite songs, and it also happened to be his birthday. I was also having one of my best rides ever.

When I climbed off the bike, I started to cry from a flood of emotions. I didn't even know what I was feeling. Andrew saw this and asked me if I was OK. I named a flood of emotions from sadness to joy to pride to loss.

Not knowing what to say, he said everything that he could think in that moment, which was something like, "Congratulations, I'm sorry, that must be hard, way to go, that's understandable, and you're doing great."

I laughed through my tears. He said, "I'm sorry, I want to say the right thing, but I don't know what it is." I told him that *that* was the right thing to say.

It's crazy to even think of what our life was like before. It doesn't even seem real.

It's been over four years since we reunited, and when our kids ask us about this period in our family history, we talk openly and honestly with them about it.

We don't hide it from people (obviously … it's in this book).

We talk about it every so often together when it's relevant, and it makes us hold one another even more closely. The appreciation for what we have and what we have been through to get here fills our hearts every day.

We feel so lucky to have what we have. I'm no relationship expert, and we continue to learn and grow every day. But I can share our recipe for what is working for us.

1. **Relationships are a place to give.** If we are both looking for opportunities to give and delight one another often, we will feel connected, fulfilled, and happy.

   That doesn't have to mean giving really big and expensive things.

   For us, in the last twenty-four hours as I write this, he went out of his way to make me laugh, which I would argue should have been included as a love language in Gary Chapman's book, because I'm pretty sure it would be my number one.

   How did he make me laugh, you ask? This time it was by showing me Jim Carrey's cameo in his own movie, *Liar Liar*, as one of his own characters, Fire Marshal Bill. Andrew is always curating things and stories to make me laugh. It makes me feel loved, warm, connected and happy.

   One of his favorite things is communication through music. I happened to come across Beyoncé's "Smash into You" (Live – PCM Stereo Version) video, and it made me think of exactly the way I feel about him when I am away from him, even if for only a day. I sent it to him.

   These small things are free, and they say, "I love you, I am thinking about you, I *know* you, I spend time on you, you matter to me, my heart is with you."

2. **Marriage first, kids second.** Kids do not come first, or the marriage will suffer, wilt, and die. The way to make kids feel safe, secure, and loved is to have two parents who love each other, who focus on caring and nurturing each other, and who lead by example, showing what healthy relationships look like so their kids can understand what that is and experience something similar.

3. **Be present.** We are very deliberate each day to be present with one another. If the other is speaking, we work to provide our undivided attention, and if we can't, we save it for when we can, which we both make an effort to come back to.

4. **Constant physical connection.** We are physically affectionate throughout each and every day as much as we can without being gross in front of the children. And even then, for fun we'll cross the lines just to purposely gross them out.

5. **Outcome-driven arguments.** We agree that the purpose of an argument isn't to be right or to drive a wedge. It is to understand one another better and to come even closer together through that understanding. Once we've stated our case, we move to a different place in our heart to listen and understand—or at least we strive to, but it's never perfect. It's usually messy, but it's *always* honest because we deserve honesty—even when it's messy.

Things we never do in an argument:

- Name-calling

- Verbally/physically abuse each other

- Walk away prematurely to avoid tough conversations. Sometimes space is required, but that only happens when both parties agree to take a break, cool off, and know that we will come back to it (vs. sweeping it under the rug). We rarely do this; we feel it's better to stay in it and work to a conclusion, but sometimes space is required.

  □ Silent treatment

6. **Be playful.** It's serious, but it's not that serious. This is actually one of our core family values. We are very playful as often as it is appropriate. With each other. With our kids and about ourselves. In work. With our extended family. With our friends.

7. **Don't take things personally.** Whenever we're in *any* relationship trying to solve an issue, we need to make it be about the issue, not about us. If someone's leaving dirty dishes out, the issue is the dirty dishes, not about the person or whether they care/don't care or whatever other ridiculous meaning we assign to such trivial issues. Just get on the same page about the protocol for dishes and *move on.*

That's it. That's all I've got on that. We're still learning, and we know our marriage is a deliberate work in progress. It's a journey I'm so grateful and honored to be on with him.

While my personal life was getting even better and better, my professional life was also improving, but I still felt like I had a long way to go.

I shared with a couple of colleagues that I was ready to seek my own next level of professional growth, and that's when I was introduced to Vistage.

Vistage is a CEO peer group where the CEOs would get together for one full day each month to learn, grow, and solve issues together. I was positive that *this* was going to be the place that I would find all the entrepreneurial answers I needed. I applied, qualified, and joined.

Joining Vistage was one of the most intimidating things I'd ever done. I was pretty sure that each leader in the group represented companies far larger than mine; they had MBAs and a world of experience that I did not. That being said, it's exactly why I wanted to be there. I'd read a quote once that said, "If you're the biggest fish in the pond, you're probably in the wrong pond." In this case, I felt like I was a minnow, and this was the ocean.

When we join the group at our first meeting, we are asked to give a brief introduction of ourselves.

I decided I was going to be as honest, open, and transparent as possible about where I came from, what I knew, and what I didn't know, even though I knew I could impress them with statistics about how we'd grown from *x* to *y* or how we innovated or won awards. Impressing them wasn't the outcome I needed. What I needed was for them to understand what I did not know so that they could help me.

Rarely did I speak from writing on a paper. By this point, I had thousands of hours of public speaking under my belt for audiences of over 500 people, did regular smaller speaking/training sessions, and always seemed to find my way to the stage or the front of the room. I was always comfortable there, but this was different. I needed to be certain that I covered every detail that I needed them to know within the allotted time frame to be considerate and not go on like a babbling nervous idiot, which I am certain I would have done had I not read from my paper.

I shared with them what type of business we had and what we did for our clients. I shared a few numbers to help them understand the size of our business, and then I shared with them the truth about the fact that I started in our business at the age of seventeen not because I was an entrepreneurial prodigy, but because I was fifteen when I had my son and I needed to go to work. I shared with them that I was very intimidated by them and imagined that they all had impressive education and work histories.

I started to share with them that I dropped out of high school, but I had to stop talking because I could feel the tears welling up in my eyes and my throat beginning to close.

I just sat with it for a moment to try to regain my composure. I took a breath and went on to share through my tears that I was able to obtain my GED and had one college class under my belt because that's all it took for me to realize that college was going to be too slow a path for me.

I let them know, though, that I valued education and worked obsessively to learn through reading, exposing myself to constant, new learning in business, and that I listened to every business podcast I could find. I shared that I received mentorship from Dan Tyre, director of sales at HubSpot, received Tony Robbins coaching, and that I'd attended hundreds of hours of business and leadership training. I shared that Vistage was my next step in education and that anything that they could share with me or teach me would be appreciated.

Finishing my introduction, I put my paper down and said, "That's it. That's me."

Everyone stood up and started clapping. That caught me off guard. It made me feel really welcomed into the group. I appreciated that so much.

I wish I could say it calmed my insecurities, but I knew I was in for a lot of learning ahead. I knew I was headed for another round of conscious incompetence. Yay.

Sharing that much of myself openly and honestly was about efficiency, and it was one of the riskiest business decisions I'd ever made. The others in the group could have pulled my Vistage Chair aside and asked him why he invited this Mickey Mouse Kid into their prominent group, and I could have been kicked out for it, as far as I knew.

I did it because I felt like we needed help and fast. We had hit a ceiling, and I could feel it every day, and it was driving me crazy. I knew there had to be a better way, and this was going to be the group that helped me find it.

After a few meetings, a peer of mine (who is now my current Vistage Chair) challenged me on what I didn't know regarding finance while I was processing an issue with the group. This was precisely why I joined Vistage … seeking out my areas of unconscious incompetence to raise them into my consciousness. And as usual, it sucked.

I realized I needed more business finance training. I signed up for the four-day MBA offered by Keith Cunningham, who I learned about business finance from at Business Mastery. He was such a fantastic teacher that I knew I would make it to his course one day, and this was going to be the day.

I knew it was going to be a stretch for me to ask to attend Keith's course, considering months before I'd just argued for the expense to sign myself up for Vistage. I made my case; thankfully the team agreed, and off I went.

When I returned, I took what I learned, brought it back, and started to train my entire company on everything I'd learned. It was brilliant education, and I highly recommend it. But somehow, while the lessons were valuable and helped us move the needle, we were still stuck.

I didn't know what I was in search of exactly, but I did know that I still hadn't found it.

In Vistage, a number of my peers were talking in almost every meeting about EOS, which I soon learned stands for the Entrepreneurial Operating System.

They connected me to their EOS Implementer to learn more and encouraged me to read *Traction* by Gino Wickman, which I did.

When I read the book, I felt like someone was peering into my business and was describing the exact pains and issues we were having. It was crazy. I shared it with my team and got approval to reach out to an EOS Implementer to learn more. When she described what EOS was and how it worked, I knew it was exactly what I'd been looking for.

With an Implementer leading us through EOS, we would have external leadership and accountability to help us take all of the very best parts of every business book I'd read and use them to help us to finally get where I thought we should be able to go.

What we learned was that we all had a vision for where the company should go on our leadership team. There was no lack of vision. The issue was that it wasn't precisely the same vision. With EOS, we created a vision together, and it was a phenomenal experience.

With her guidance, we would get to the right structure and finally solve some tough questions that we'd been facing, like how our dad might successfully exit the business and then what comes after, and other big operational issues, like how do we transition out of a CRM that had been financially strenuous and create our own proprietary program? Or how do we determine if that's even the right move?

We would finally get into the right meetings and ensure we were solving the *right* problems each week, quarter, and year. Reid Hoffman (founder of LinkedIn) said once on his podcast *Masters of Scale* that to be an entrepreneur means that there are little fires burning everywhere all the time, and our job as the leaders of those organizations is to get better at knowing which fires to tackle and which fires to let burn.

EOS gave us tools to be able to assess that accurately and consistently.

It also gave us very clear, black and white ways for us to know if we had the right people on the bus, and if they were in the right seats. It's a concept popularized by Jim Collins, but how do you know for certain if/when this an issue? It's not always so obvious and it's often something we manage based on feeling and emotion rather than data. I heard Gary Vaynerchuk give some incredibly sage advice to entrepreneurial leaders on going straight back to their offices from the conference he was speaking at, and he told them to assess who the toxic people were in their organization and then do something about it.

The *"how"* on this is what evades people, in my experience. And EOS has a brilliant, simple, black-and-white way to assess the right people in an organization, helping move these very difficult discussions forward.

With our new EOS structure, there was 100 percent transparency and accountability, and because of it, we were crushing in one year what we thought we might not be able to do in three years pre-EOS.

Because of our great work and synergy together, even though revenues went down one year, cash went up. The organization was operating more efficiently.

Because of our outstanding results, we felt prepared and able to sell the business in October 2020 to a strategic buyer at above-market multiples and with all of us original owners landing exactly where we wanted to be.

Our company, Western Asset Protection, is still running on EOS, and my brother Paul is still leading the charge within the organization.

> My life today is exactly everything that I imagined it could be, and I feel like it's only just beginning.

My life today is exactly everything that I imagined it could be, and I feel like it's only just beginning, considering I just turned forty.

I credit my new reality to a commitment to constantly learn and grow but especially to the massive shift in our business and my life, which I'm certain wouldn't have happened without EOS.

I'm grateful every day to Gino Wickman, Don Tinney, and all of the original EOS Implementers that had the strength to bring this incredible system out into the world to improve and enrich the lives of so many and get it to where it is today, with over 10,000 companies running on it.

EOS also happens to be in perfect alignment with my goal to help as many people achieve as great a life as possible, whatever fulfillment looks like to them, which is why my day job is as an EOS Implementer.

And while I get to help entrepreneurial leaders run a better business so that they can live even better lives, my mission is not just for entrepreneurs or even leaders in business.

Which brings me to the second part of my mission, which is to help anyone who has a desire to define what success and fulfillment looks like and be able to do it, regardless of experience, education, gender, skin color, or location in the world.

Your life is so precious to me. I hope it is to you, too, and that you take this opportunity to take these next steps to make sure that your time here is everything you want it to be.

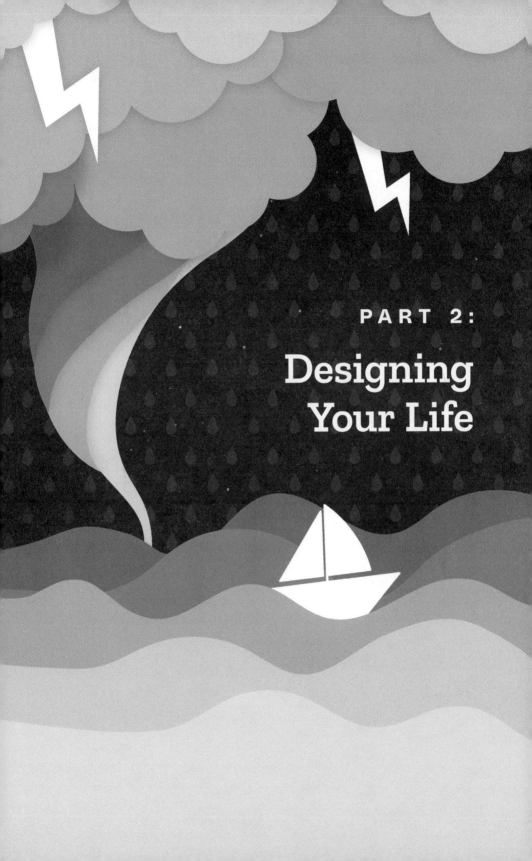

PART 2:

# Designing
# Your Life

# AN INTRODUCTION TO
# Designing Your Life

The first time I did an exercise like this, to imagine what I wanted for my life, I was excited. Imagine me sitting at a Tony Robbins event with my notebook on my lap, my lanyard around my neck, and surrounded by a bunch of other people crazy enough to attend one of these life changing events.

Bright-eyed and optimistic about the idea that I could create my own destiny, this is about how the conversation went in my head:

*"Ohhh! This is exciting. OK. Whaaat doo I waant?"* (That's me writing down the question … vowels get drawn out when I write about writing words.)

My head flooded with images of various aspects of my life, but I couldn't seem to zero in on any one thing.

*"OK … focus, Mari, focus! What do I want? Come on! This is the moment that I get to really design my life. Think. Think. Thiiink!*

*"I know for sure that I want to have financial peace. I mean, I don't need to be a billionaire or anything, just to be financially free. Not that I'd not want to be a billionaire. I don't want to not attract that somehow. OK. What else do I want? I definitely want to be in the best shape of my life. What else, what else? I want a really great marriage and relationships with my kids. I want to have more time for friends and social things in my life."*

I was having trouble. Naming what I thought my life could look like ended up being harder than I expected, and if I am honest, there was a new thought and feeling creeping up inside:

What if I name what I want for my life, but I'm not able to achieve it? What if I don't have what it takes to make it happen?

Then I walked all the way down that path in my head. Knowing what I envisioned but not being able to achieve it meant a tortured life knowing I had this amazing vision that was too far for me to reach, and that I would be stuck with the reality that it will never come true.

In my head I even made it all the way to my deathbed with all my regrets laid out in front of me and then dramatically expiring with a long, drawn-out, final exhale of breath.

So yeah. This is super fun. This exercise just turned into pain and fear of failure. Why on earth would I want to set myself up for failure?

For me, the fork in the road of whether I should move forward boiled down to one word.

Responsibility.

I am the only one who is responsible for making sure my time on this planet is fun, happy, meaningful, and fulfilling. No one else is going to get me to that but me.

Stephen Covey encourages us to look at the word "responsibility" as "response-ability," meaning the ability to choose your response.

He says that highly proactive people recognize that they can choose their response to things. He goes on to say, "They do not blame circumstances, conditions, or conditioning for their behavior. Their behavior is a product of their own conscious choice based on values. Rather than a product of their conditions based on feeling."

What this means is that a responsible person is someone who does not make excuses, does not blame others or circumstances for where they are or end up, and who pushes through feelings to take deliberate action.

The feelings part of this is *really* important. Responsible people, people who proactively make their lives happen, do not make decisions throughout their day based on their feelings. They base their decisions on what they said they were going to do, and they do it anyway, whether they feel like it or not. In other words, they uphold a consistent level of integrity with and for themselves as well as with those they serve.

For us to have integrity with ourselves means doing the things we said we would do—for ourselves. It's about private victories.

Having integrity with those we serve means doing the things we said we would do—for others. It's about public victories.

It's critical to master private victories first. As Tony Robbins said, "One victory in public is a result of hundreds of victories in private."

Another way to think about integrity that I love is Brené Brown's definition, which can be found in herbook *Rising Strong*, where she defines it like this:

"Integrity is choosing courage over comfort; choosing what is right over what is fun, fast, or easy; and choosing to practice our values rather than simply professing them."

Every time I read that, I take a deep breath. That's the kind of person I want to be.

We can choose to step up to the challenge of taking responsibility for our lives by working toward greater integrity with ourselves and others, or we can resign ourselves to just continue life as is.

I had fears about designing a life and not being able to achieve it, but I moved forward anyway because I shifted my focus to what I would feel like if I never even tried.

I would imagine myself sitting in a rocking chair at the end of my life and thinking back to the ideas and visions I had but decided to never pursue. What I know I would feel in that moment is regret as I realize that my time is up. There are no do-overs. That was it. And I blew it.

It's dramatic; I know. But it's how I move my current self to do nice things for my future self.

Join me in exploring what's possible for your life. If you don't believe in you, know that I do, because I'm doing it, and I'm just like you. I'm no different. I'm scared regularly. I'm battling bullshit, head-trashing voices all the time. I worry what other people think. I feel like an imposter at times, and I feel like giving up sometimes, just like anyone else. But I fight through it and am working to get to the other side.

I say join me because I'm still in it. I'm still hustling. I still haven't figured it all out. And I'm going with or without you into my ideal future, and I'm inviting you to come with me.

I can't guarantee you'll get to what you want any more than I can for myself. All I know is that I know how to get up, dust myself off, and try again. And when I try again and again, and fall again and again, 5, 50 or 1,000 times, each time I will get back up and keep going.

## 2 . 1

# Are You Ready to Create Your Dream Life?

Excellent! I am *so excited* and honored to be here doing this with you. Before we get started, there are three things I need you to know.

## 1. Your Most Valuable Resource.

The reason I was able to take my life from being a fifteen-year-old mom on welfare to a successful CEO and entrepreneur with a life even better than I could have dreamed of wasn't just because I had grit, tenacity, and self-directed education. It is because I learned to be resourceful.

In Tony Robbins's TED Talk, he asks the audience if they've ever failed to achieve something significant in their lives. Then he asked them why; what didn't they have? [1]

---

1    TED Ideas Worth Spreading, "Why We Do What We Do,"
     YouTube, Video, 21:11, February 2006, https://www.ted.com/talks/
     tony_robbins_why_we_do_what_we_do?language=en#t-419126

People start to call out money, time, technology, the right manager, and then Al Gore says, "The Supreme Court," referring to the loss of the election in 2000 to George W. Bush.

What Tony calls out is that what each of those things have in common, time, technology, and even the Supreme Court is that they are all resources. And what he argues is that it is not a lack of resources, it is a lack of *resourcefulness* that causes us to fail.

Where do we get resourcefulness?

Resourcefulness occurs when we're charged up with emotion, passion, and conviction. Tony goes on to imply that if Al Gore had only spoken with emotion and passion during his election, he would have known people who would have voted for him that did not.

In other words, there may have been no need for a recount.

My burning passion (emotion) has become my leverage to get to the life I can see for myself and my family. It has generated enough power to find ways to navigate any obstacle and find a way for anything that I want or need.

I know that there are people with even greater obstacles in front of them than others. I consider myself to be privileged in that regard. Sure, I was on welfare for a brief time and had a number of challenges, but the reality is that I speak English, I was born in the US, I have white skin and blue eyes, and I was born into an entrepreneurial family. All those things make me more privileged than many, and I fully acknowledge the unfair advantages of those things compared to what you or others may be facing.

I heard our advantages and disadvantages referred to once as a starting line in the race of life, and depending on where you are born in the world, your gender, skin color, language, race, disability, and socioeconomic status all matter in how far back you are starting in this race.

Your starting line might be farther back than so many others for any one of these reasons. So what does that mean? You shouldn't go for it? You shouldn't try? Who's winning then? Who knows? But it sure as hell won't be you. And we'll be losing, too, because we won't have your beautiful contributions in this tapestry of possibility that we all create and share together.

I say get pissed about how unfair it is. Get angry about the fact that there are people at the front of the starting line who were born with all the advantages and who have all the power.

While you're at it, I recommend gathering up anything else that sucks into this same container. Maybe the way your parents raised you or didn't raise you. Maybe the things you deserved as a kid but didn't get, including but not limited to love, safety, and having your basic needs met.

Anything else you want to stuff in there is good too. Maybe you're at a breaking point and furious about where you are in life right now. Add that too. It's all valuable.

Now. Harness it by putting that container of emotional leverage on your back, get control of it, and then *use it*.

How to do that is to understand that these emotions in your body are like nuclear energy. Uncontrolled nuclear energy can destroy a city. Uncontrolled in you, it can destroy your life. Controlled, and it can power a city. Controlled, it can fuel your life.

A perfect example of someone creating leverage through emotion is Nelson Mandela. When he was released from wrongful imprisonment after twenty-seven years, he could have started a war, and no one would have blamed him.

Instead, he leveraged his anger and platform to negotiate and end apartheid and ultimately became the first Black president of South Africa, where he could continue to do even more good for the country.

Resourcefulness comes from leverage created by emotion and, if we hope to change the world like he did, we should consciously and responsibly tap into it and then use it for good.

## It Takes as Long as It Takes.

Notice that in my story, there are no magic pills. There are no shortcuts. There is no get-rich-quick story. There is no fast track.

It took me twenty-two years to learn how to build a company and almost as long to get to healthy relationships, learn to set boundaries, and ultimately start sticking up for myself.

I'm still learning how to do better each day and don't have these things mastered. So even though Waze tells me daily I have arrived, I have not nor will I ever "arrive." There will always be opportunities to learn more, grow, and go deeper.

People often say, "It's not about the destination; it's about the journey." OK. Sure. I don't know why, but that doesn't resonate with me. Said better by my BFF Tony Robbins (hey, it could happen!), "It's not about the goal—it's about who we get to become achieving it."

Who would I have to be to achieve [*insert cool thing*]? What habits would I have to have? What kind of people would I be spending time with? What would I say no to? What would I get to say *yes* to? What would my daily routine need to include? Now *that's* all kinda fun to think about.

Enjoy the process of becoming the kind of person that can achieve what you want to achieve.

# Everything You Need Is within You Now.

If you're looking for the answers for what you should do with your life, know that they are not now nor will ever be out there. Which path to take, which relationships to keep, and which ones to leave behind: no one on this earth knows that except you.

The only way to get to these answers is by exploring, discovering, uncovering, and asking really great questions.

Also, in you is everything you need to succeed. Already. Right now. Just so we're on the same page and I'm not missing anything, I created a checklist:

> **In you is everything you need to succeed. Already. Right now.**

- You are living and breathing.

- You can communicate (verbally, signing, writing).

- You are capable of learning new things (just think back to the last time you switched from Android to Apple!).

- You are capable of doing something consistently (i.e., brushing your teeth, showering, calling your mother).

- You have a desire to achieve something, no matter how big or small.

If you have those five things, you have everything you need within you *right now* to get to wherever you want to go. All we're going to do is dial these existing powers that you have up a few notches to get you to where you want to go next.

Next, I'll give you an overview of the process, then I'll teach you how we do it, and then we'll be like Nike and "Just Do It."

# Overview

There are seven simple steps in this process.

Please do not confuse the word "simple" with the word "easy." As cliché as it is to say this, if this stuff was easy, you'd already be doing it. Everyone would be. It is critical that we keep things simple because complexity is the enemy of execution.

**Here are the 7 Simple Steps:**

- Step 1: End – Begin with the end in mind.

- Step 2: Dream – What does your dream life look like?

- Step 3: Vision – Bring that dream closer into an actionable vision.

- Step 4: Plan – What do you need to do in the next twelve months?

- Step 5: Rocks – What needs to happen in the next ninety days?

- Step 6: Scoreboard – Activities to do consistently each week.

- Step 7: Lists – A place to store *all* the things we can't do today.

There are two ways to complete this program. There's the DIY or Do It Yourself way, or there's the DIWU which is the Do It With Us way (so dorky, I know) which you can learn more about on my website at maritautimes.com. If you opt for the DIY way, before you do any of this work, I highly recommend leaving your normal environment for each exercise. Go to a park, coffee shop, library, coworking space, anywhere that isn't your home or office. When you get there, let people know you are 100 percent unavailable during this time. Turn your phone on airplane mode, take off your smartwatch, and do all of your exercises on paper. You can transfer it to digital later. Your life deserves 100 percent of your attention and focus.

Regarding how long this entire process takes, it depends on if you opt to do one exercise a week for seven weeks or if you do them all in a day or two, depending on where you are in your journey.

I also try to tell you how long it takes to do each exercise individually, but that can of course vary, too, depending on whether you're a high fact finder (like my husband) or a quick start (like me) according to the Kolbe assessment. Or if you're a Specialist (like my husband) or a Maverick (like me) according to the Predictive Index.

Speaking of which, these are both assessments we've taken so that we might "know thyself" better, which I think is a critical step in the process of getting to a great life.

There are so many assessments: Enneagram, Myers-Briggs, DISC, EQ, etc. … they're all different and valuable, and they'll tell you what you already know, but they give you language to be able to tell others, too, and to be better at predicting what we'll need to get things done in our lives.

But as usual, I digress.

So let's get you going on your journey to your dream life.

# Step 1: End

**The Point:** Begin with the end in mind

**Time:** 30 minutes

**Materials:** PDFs @ maritautimes.com or any notebook will do. Where we'll begin is at the end.

I learned the importance of this from Stephen Covey. He tells us that we should begin with the end in mind to be crystal clear about what it is we want to accomplish in our lives.

What he recommends is that we walk ourselves down the aisle of our own funerals. I know that sounds so morose, but it's a really useful exercise, so stick with me.

He asks us to consider: who is there to pay their respects? What impact or influence did we have in their lives? What kinds of things are they saying about us?

The value in thinking about the end of our life is like spending time thinking about our core values. Both serve as a compass or a decision filter. We can run decisions we're about to make through these filters to answer questions or solve problems in a way that helps us stay true to ourselves and our mission in life.

You can go to the website and download the PDF for these exercises, or you can write the questions out on your own page and answer them.

After you've written your answers down, take the time to evaluate what you wrote. What needs to happen in your life because of what you discovered? What are you not doing now that you need to? What are you doing now that you need to stop?

As you answer, don't assume you'll be living another forty years and have time on your side to get it right. While I hope we all have many years ahead of us, we don't know how long we have, and getting these things done and started is more of a priority than you might think.

## Step 2: Dream

**The Point:** Get inspired and create your ultimate life vision

**Time:** 2 hours

**Materials:**

1. PDFs @ maritautimes.com or any notebook will do.

2. Guided Meditation @ maritautimes.com

The first thing we're going to do is venture into the world of possibility, imagination, and creativity by dreaming.

We'll start by asking you to name people in your life that you admire, value, and maybe even aspire to be more like. When you see them, you might feel energized and inspired. You might already work to emulate them, or sometimes you might wish you had characteristics like them, or maybe you already do.

We'll break these folks into three categories. Famous people, teachers/mentors, and friends/peers.

Famous people: I enjoy seeing what other people do for their lives and find it inspiring. Some of my favorites are Beyoncé, Tony Robbins, Dwayne Johnson, Jess King, Tim Ferriss, Brené Brown, Dave Chappelle, Gary Vaynerchuk, Oprah Winfrey, Sara Bareilles, or insert any other mega, larger-than-life figure. Do you have people like that you admire? If so, write down as many of them that you can think of.

If you can't think of anyone, skip to the next step. Not everyone digs famous peeps, and that's OK.

Teachers/mentors: Next, consider who helped shaped how you think about the world and who you go to when you want to learn. They could be parents, teachers, mentors, employers/bosses, or other people you've looked to for advice and guidance that you admire.

Friends/peers: Finally, consider your friends and peer network. Who stands out as someone that you respect, appreciate, and maybe even wish to emulate?

List them all out. As many as you can think of.

Next, circle the top three people. *I know*! That will be hard to do, but it's important. If you had to pick your top three, who would it be? You could pick one from each category or pick all three from one, but only name three.

Finally, thinking of those three people, what is it that you like about them or their lives?

If you're using the PDF from the website, work in one question at a time while thinking of all three people. If you're working from your own paper, write the three questions listed below and then do the same thing by thinking of all three people and answering the questions.

Questions:

1.  How do they behave? What characteristics do you admire? For example, maybe they always do what they say they are going to do. Or maybe they listen really well or are dedicated to their marriage.

2.  What kinds of things do they have?

3.  How do they spend their time? What do they prioritize?

Now … it's time to back into what you want to be about. It's neat to see what other people do, but it should only be a source of inspiration and help you spark ideas.

We're working to get to who the best version of *you* is and what is possible for *your* life. Defining what you uniquely value. We are not being our authentic selves if we're aiming our goals at what other people have accomplished. We just use it to spark ideas and inspiration.

So now that you've got some fun ideas rattling around in your brain, I want to tap into that even further. I want to pry into an even deeper level of what you see through a guided meditation.

This guided meditation was specifically formulated for this purpose and is conducted by Ashley Gibbs Davis, who is a leadership coach, has an MBA from Yale University, and is a Brené Brown Dare to Lead Facilitator. I chose her for this meditation because she knows the hearts of people on a mission to achieve things and has an incredible capacity to guide people into their hearts and out of their heads, which is where I think our vision needs to really come from.

Please pause here and go to my website, maritautimes.com, to locate the guided meditation. Complete the associated PDF with it there.

# Step 3: Vision

**The Point:** Bring your dream down into a defined vision
**Time:** 2 hours–2 weeks
**Materials:** PDFs @ maritautimes.com

You've now defined what your dream life would look like. It might take you ten years to get to that vision; it might take you thirty. It doesn't matter. It's a clearly stated picture of what you think life could ultimately be like, and it's exciting to think about.

With that clarity, now what we want to do is to back that into an inspiring upcoming milestone. Something that we might be looking forward to, like an event or a birthday. When I was thirty-three, I realized the upcoming milestone of thirty-five and decided to set that time difference as my goal. It's whatever you want it to be. Make it up, make it inspiring, and *set it*! It should be something that's around eighteen to twenty-four months away or more.

Define that time frame for you and then write that date at the top of your page.

To help provide an example and context, we'll use my friend Clementine's goals as an example. She goes by Clem. We're only going to use one of her goals as an example, but you'll ultimately want to pick between one to three to work on.

Clem said her milestone is eighteen months from now on her fortieth birthday, which is October 1, 2023.

In the category of finance, Clem wants to:

- Be 100 percent debt free

- Have $400K in savings
- Earn $200K a year
- Own her home free and clear

To know what she might be able to get done by October 1, 2023, Clem will need to assess where she is now. After some research, she discovers that she is currently:

- $40K in debt
- Has $100K in savings
- Earns $135K a year
- Has a $235K mortgage

Based on that information and after some further calculations, she discovers that by October 1, 2023, she can get to:

- $12K in debt paid down
- $12K in savings added
- Certification completed to reach next promotional level

# Step 4: Plan

**The Point:** Define what needs to get done in the next twelve months

**Time:** 2 hours

**Materials:** PDFs @ maritautimes.com

Very simply, we'll break her eighteen-month dream down into a twelve-month plan.

Again, we start with a date. For her, it's April 1, 2022.

Her goals for the year related to finance would be:

- $8K in debt paid
- $8K in savings achieved
- 4 certification modules completed

# Step 5: Rocks

**The Point:** Define what needs to get done in the next ninety days

**Time:** 2 hours

**Materials:** PDFs @ maritautimes.com

Stephen Covey popularized Eisenhower's time management matrix in his book *The 7 Habits of Highly Effective People*. When Eisenhower created it, he said that "managing time itself is no longer the aim, but managing where to focus at any particular time."[2] See the diagram below.

## TIME MANAGEMENT MATRIX

| | URGENT | NOT URGENT |
|---|---|---|
| **IMPORTANT** | **1**<br>• Crises<br>• Emergencies<br>• Pressing problems<br>• Deadline-driven projects<br>• Last-minute preparations | **2**<br>• Preparation, planning, prevention<br>• Values clarification<br>• Capabilities improvement<br>• Relationship building<br>• True recreation/relaxation |
| **NOT IMPORTANT** | **3**<br>• Interruptions<br>• Some callers, some mail<br>• Some meetings<br>• Many pressing matters<br>• Popular activities | **4**<br>• Busy work<br>• Trivial activities<br>• Some calls/emails<br>• Escape activities<br>• Time wasters |

---

2   Francisco Saez, "The Time Management Matrix," FacileThings.com, accessed August 2, 2021, https://facilethings.com/blog/en/time-management-matrix.

In the top left quadrant (Quadrant 1), we have things that are urgent and important. If someone is having a heart attack in front of you, it is both urgent and important, and it must be dealt with now.

In the top right quadrant (Quadrant 2), we have things that are not urgent but important. This would be things like reading, working out, spending time thinking about how you might delight your loved ones, and real rest and relaxation.

In the bottom left quadrant (Quadrant 3), we have the not urgent but important; these might be other people's urgencies that they're trying to hand off to you to do. Hand them back.

And in the bottom right quadrant (Quadrant 4), we have the not urgent and not important. I call this the "Netflix and Chill" category, and I love it. Sometimes we need that time too.

Of the four quadrants, Quadrant 2 (important, not urgent) is where "Rock" work fits. We use the term "Rocks" in EOS to help businesses set their priorities for the quarter. I'd been doing this kind of work on my own life for years before this but didn't think to call them Rocks. I love it.

It's based on the well-known concept that if you had a glass jar, and the jar represented all of your time, and just outside of the jar you had rocks, pebbles, sand, and water, the order in which you put those items in the jar matters. In short—the only way to fit everything in the jar is to put the rocks first. But by nature, they are not urgent because they live in Quadrant 2. So we need to create urgency around them by making them priorities with deadlines.

My favorite video that brings together Quadrant 2, the things that are important not urgent, and Rock concepts can be found by googling "Rocks, Pebbles, and Sand Story." It's about a two-minute-long video to watch.

We use it in our businesses, and we'll use it here, too, because it's brilliant.

Now, we need to set your Rocks (priorities) for the next ninety days based on what you said you wanted to get done this year.

Using Clem's example, what does she need to get done in the next ninety days to achieve her twelve-month plan? Whatever the answers are to that will be our Rocks.

We'll break it down, but first I want to set a Rock-setting rule, because when we go to create it, we want to make sure that we make it specific, measurable, attainable, relatable, and timely. If you like acronyms, that spells SMART.

We'll do that by taking Clem's twelve-month goals and dividing them into four quarters. Twelve months divided by four quarters = three months per quarter.

We refresh and reset our goals every quarter, which happens to be around the same times that the world naturally refreshes its seasons.

If her goal is to pay down $8K of debt and increase savings by $8K over twelve months, all she needs to do is divide that by four to know what she'd need to accomplish in the next ninety days to reach her goal.

- $8K in debt / 4 quarters = $2K per quarter

- $8K in savings / 4 quarters = $2K per quarter

- 4 courses / 4 quarters = 1 course

But let's say that about the same time of her setting this first set of goals, she starts attending Dave Ramsey's Financial Peace University at www.ramseysolutions.com where she learns she has enough savings already to get her through an emergency, so if she instead applied all her funds to her debt, she'd be able to pay it off even faster and start saving faster.

So she decides instead to apply all $4K in funds to her debt.

Her Rock deadline date is going to be July 1, 2022.

She names her first Rock: have $4K in high-interest debt paid down, and her second Rock: complete one certification course.

Now, let's check our SMART standards.

**S**pecific: Yes.

**M**easurable: Yes, $4K and one certification course are the measurements.

**A**ttainable: Yes, we checked with our money and time budgets.

**R**elatable: They tie into what she hopes to achieve long term.

**T**imely: Yes, we set a date of June 30, 2022.

Next, Clem will want to break down each Rock into steps we'll call milestones, which are shorter to-dos with due dates to be clear on what success will be on the way to accomplishing the Rock.

She decides her milestones are as follows:

First Rock: Have $4K in high-interest debt paid down.

- Budget established and achieving 90 percent-plus meeting it. (Due: 4/7/2022)

- Consolidate debt to lower interest card (Due: 4/16/2022)

- Sell second car (Due: 4/30/2022)

- Drive for Uber (Due: 5/15/2022)

- Sell baseball cards (Due: 7/30/2022)

Second Rock: One certification completed

- Sign up for certification course (Due: 5/1/2022)

- Schedule time to work on it each week (Due: 5/1/2022)

This all looks spastic in a book layout, so go to my website at maritautimes.com to see what it looks like in our formatted PDF, and you'll see the breakdown easier.

# Step 6: Scoreboard

**The Point:** Measure weekly activity to stay on track

**Time:** 1 hour

**Materials:** PDFs @ maritautimes.com

Keith Cunningham taught us that in business, if we don't know how to read the scoreboard, we don't know how to win the game.

No game is won by a single giant play. It's not even won solely by what's happening on the field. It's hundreds and thousands of little things that add up during the pregame preparation as well. Each incremental move is adding up to significant progress.

That's our weekly scoreboard. The very small and incremental things we're doing each week to add up to *massive* shifts and change in our lives.

Looking at Clem's Rocks, she decides to set her scoreboard up like this:

| WEEKLY SCOREBOARD | | | | | |
|---|---|---|---|---|---|
| Goal (or TD) | Week 1 | Week 2 | Week 3 | Week 4 | Week 5 |
| 2+ hrs. on $$ | 4 | 2 | 1 | 1.5 | 3 |
| 1+ hr. on cert. | 3 | 1 | 2 | 1 | 1 |

If you think the goal is to hit 100 percent, you would be incorrect. 100 percent is perfect, and perfect is the lowest standard a person can set for themselves because it is an impossible one.

We're just stuck on 100 percent because that's what school told us was the goal. We're not in school. We're in life.

For our tests in school, we studied, prepared, our friends were studying and preparing for the same thing, and it was 100 percent our only priority and focus with total accountability to our teachers and guardians. Sure. 100 percent as the goal there makes sense.

In life, what we want to aim for is forward progress, and if we're achieving these things at 80 percent or better, we're more than likely 100 percent better off than we were before we did this really great work. So there. There's our 100 percent.

> In life, what we want to aim for is forward progress.

When you do this for the first time, you might be tempted to add a bunch of numbers that you may not need to track on the scoreboard. You might be this person if you sometimes write out lists of things that need to get done and then add a few things you already did so you can check them off too.

The scoreboard is to track two types of activities:

1.  Specific Rock to work this quarter

2.  Activities that you would like to become future habits

Once these things become habit, doing these things just becomes a part of who you are. It becomes your new identity.

Our identity is made up of a lot of things, but mostly it's formed by the habits we've developed over the years. Those habits become our norm, our comfort zone. Our body's version of our room temperature.

The older we get, the more hardwired they become, and the automated parts of our brains and bodies work to support them subconsciously to keep us comfortable in that temperature range.

That means that our conscious, thinking brain can be dead-on hitting a target (that's you planning, filling out your scoreboard, and telling others your plans), but our subconscious brain and body are far more powerful than you thought and will work to keep you at room temperature.

If you ever hear someone say, "I'm just the type of person that has to work out five days a week." This is their identity, and they have a powerful, subconscious driving force in their brains and bodies that helps them to maintain that identity. So working out actually isn't that difficult or as difficult for them to maintain as other people.

This is, of course, also true for a person who says, "I'm just not the type of person that works out." The same forces are at play, and the same subconscious systems will work to continue to make that true. It will be significantly harder for this person to shift into a new identity if that's what they want to do, but not impossible. It can be done, but it has to be chipped away at consistently to reprogram. To rewire. Hence the scoreboard.

There's an outstanding show on Gaia from Amazon Prime called *Rewired* by Dr. Joe Dispenza, which explains the science of how this works and what you can do about it.

# Step 7: Issues Lists

**The Point:** See everything & parking lots

**Time:** 1 hour

**Materials:** PDFs @ maritautimes.com

An issues list is an EOS tool that has changed my life. It is so simple and so powerful.

In EOS, we have two types of issues lists, a short term (weekly) and a long term (quarterly/annual). These lists serve as parking lots for issues, which we identify as ideas, conversations, problems, and opportunities that we might want to consider.

What these lists boil down to is focus and efficiency.

Focus: Because we aren't getting distracted and pulled away from what we already predicted our most important priorities were. But we can also have confidence and comfort knowing that all the things we might want to work on are parked in a spot that is easy to refer back to.

Efficiency: When we're not being distracted by shiny objects, we're able to continue to do deep and good work. When we do go to look at the list and discuss/solve anything that's on it, we can clearly see what the priority is because it's all listed out vs. guessing at what we might need to work on.

How often has your current self paid the price of your past self by overcommitting and trying to tackle too many things at once? What was the result of that? How did it make you feel when you couldn't follow through on something? The only way to have integrity and do what we say is to do fewer things better.

But the reason people overcommit is understandable. If a person doesn't have a set of decision filters, like having a dream, vision, plan, Rocks, milestones, and scoreboards, they don't know what the most important things are.

If people don't have an issues list to store things that they can't do today, they feel pressure to do everything today.

Following this system and process, you will now have new decision filters to help operate your life.

## Staying on Track

In EOS, we have what we call a Meeting Pulse. The purpose of this is to keep our leadership teams on track each week, quarter, and year with what they said they wanted to accomplish.

Running our lives isn't so different from running a business, and it deserves a similar level of attention.

Each week, on the same day, at the same time, we need to sit down and review our Rocks and milestones and take the time to put in the good work that will need to be done.

Each quarter, we need to evaluate if we've hit our goals, celebrate our accomplishments, and then reset for the new quarter.

Each year, we need to look at our dream, reset our vision if appropriate, and then create a new plan with new Rocks.

These meetings are the number one indicator if these goals will or will not be achieved. They're critical. More on how to conduct these meetings at maritautimes.com.

## How Much Time Do You Really Have?

Your future self will really love it if your current self could properly assess how much time you actually have.

I have a tool on my website at maritautimes.com, or you can recreate it yourself. It's simple. Take your twenty-four-hour day and subtract the time you spend sleeping, commuting, working, eating, etc. Do the same for the weekend.

How many hours are left to work on your Rocks and scoreboard items?

Looking at your list, what things might you need to stop doing to create more time? What things could you delegate to someone else?

I have someone clean my house every other week. That's enough for us, and we clean up the rest of the time. It costs me $400/month. I recapture twenty hours (five hours every weekend) to work on my life, rest, or play. And they do a much better job anyway.

If you're not able to hire someone, then do what I used to do before I could, and spend that five hours learning and growing at the same time. Tony Robbins talks about NET time—or "No Extra Time."

Some people tell me they can't listen to audio books, because they don't retain it or because they can't make notes. I say find a way to get it in somehow, physical book or otherwise. And I'm sorry. That's the only way I can fit it in.

My only suggestion would be to keep trying. Maybe it's something that can be developed. Or maybe the books you were listening to weren't that inspiring to you or your journey.

Remember our chat about resourcefulness earlier? This is where it comes into play. Think through *all* of the ways you can get these things done to get yourself to the next level. If you want it bad enough, you'll figure it out.

## Next Steps

I don't know about you, but I read books like this and think, "*Yes*! Great ideas!" And with all of the good intention in the world, I mean to go to the websites and download the PDFs or do the exercises, but I rarely ever do. But occasionally I do, and it changes my life. I hope this is one of those instances for you.

It is so important to me to see you succeed that I want to support you personally. Go to my website at maritautimes.com and get engaged. My team and I are working diligently to figure out how to make all of this accessible and doable for *anyone* that wants to take their life to the next level.

## Why the Time Is Now!

If your life was a book, consider that the first half (meaning everything up until now, regardless of your age) was written *for* you. It's the circumstances you were born into, the education you received, the family that surrounded you, the friendships you fell into (for lack of a better word), and the beliefs that you were given.

The second half of your life, or the second half of your book, is filled with blank pages just waiting for you to write in them. On these pages, you get to define what your circumstances are going to be, now and in the future, the education you want to receive, the amount of time you spend with which family members, which friendships you might want to develop intentionally, and the new beliefs that you decide are true for you.

Those blank pages are filled with risk and vulnerability because you are stepping into something new, and doing something new for the first time is always a vulnerable experience.

And if you think that to be vulnerable is some type of weakness, here is the definition:

> vul·ner·a·ble: the quality or state of being exposed to the possibility of being attacked or harmed, either physically or emotionally.

Stepping out into the unknown literally elicits the same emotions and feelings as being attacked. So no, being vulnerable is not an act of weakness. It is actually the opposite. To make yourself vulnerable is the ultimate act of courage. It means that even though you were afraid of being exposed or harmed, you *did it anyway.*

In Brené Brown's book *Daring Greatly*, she quotes Teddy Roosevelt's famous speech, Citizenship in a Republic, that is now more commonly called The Man in the Arena.

In it he says:

> It is not the critic who counts; not the man who points out how the strong man stumbles, or where the doer of deeds could have done them better. The credit belongs to the man who is actually in the arena, whose face is marred by dust and sweat and blood; who strives valiantly; who errs,

who comes short again and again, because there is no effort without error and shortcoming; but who does actually strive to do the deeds; who knows great enthusiasms, the great devotions; who spends himself in a worthy cause; who at the best knows in the end the triumph of high achievement, and who at the worst, if he fails, at least fails while daring greatly, so that his place shall never be with those cold and timid souls who neither know victory nor defeat.

Defining your own path is to put yourself in the middle of the arena in the boxing match of your life, and everyone is in the stands watching.

> **To get in the ring, you are guaranteed to know both defeat and victory.**

To get in the ring, you are guaranteed to know both defeat and victory.

The alternative is to sit in the stands eating popcorn and cotton candy along with all of the other timid souls, watching and maybe even judging everyone else who had the guts to get in the ring.

If you decide to take these next steps, I encourage you to explore all things Brené Brown along your journey, starting with her TED Talk. With her work, you will be able to find comfort in the discomfort, or as she calls it, "the suck." Because there will be parts that suck. There will also be parts that are exhilarating and will make you feel more alive than you've ever felt before.

## Setting Yourself up for Success

There is no straight road to success. Not for anything worth getting after. So expect bumps and slips and setbacks to occur. Some people say it's God or the universe just testing to see how bad you want it.

I just say that *obviously* there will be setbacks and hardships and bumps in the road, because this is hard work. And as my mentor, Dan Tyre, reminds me often, hard things are hard.

To make any massive change, there are tons of psychological tips and tricks to know. There are books you can read. There are blogs you can follow. There are YouTube videos you can watch. You can put Post-It Notes up in your bathroom. And keep your running shoes out, cut up your credit cards, and buy new gear.

You can say "I am" statements and watch *Rewired* by Dr. Joe Dispenza. You can read *The 7 Habits of Highly Effective People* by Stephen Covey and *Succeed: How We Can Reach Our Goals* by Dr. Heidi Halvorson and listen to *The GaryVee Audio Experience* or Brendon Burchard's, or *How I Built This* with Guy Raz and *Masters of Scale* with Reid Hoffman. Figure out your "why" with Simon Sinek and attend a Tony Robbins seminar.

My answer to *all* of that is *yes*. Do *all* of those things *over time* (not all at once) and keep searching for new things. Be sure to listen to people that resonate with you, not just who I talk about.

It will take more than one approach, more than one time, and more than one tip. Everything you can do and read and listen to will be good for creating your very best life.

What's equally important is what you're keeping *out* of your head and heart. Jim Rohn shared with us the importance of standing guard at the door of our minds. Do not let toxic people, shows, songs, and newsfeeds invade your precious brain. Define what that means for you and constantly stand guard.

So when you hit those inevitable snags, welcome them. Be playful and just say, "Oh, there you are you little [*insert your degree of language*]. Now ... what am I going to do with you?" Stay in control, recognize that it's par for the course, and make a conscious decision.

Understand that this is one of those "response-ability" moments that we learned from Stephen Covey. You have the ability to take a moment to think, reflect, and respond in the *new* way that you are working to live and be.

You created a vision for your future self, and the only way to get to that version of you in the future is to start responding like they would *right now*.

## Don't Go It Alone

If this is something that you decide to do on your own, that's super; just make sure you tell someone and make the commitment to them, because according to the American Society of Training and Development,[3] you have a 65 percent chance of completing this goal if you at least share it with someone else and commit to them.

If you want to increase your chance of success by up to 95 percent, you'll want to set a specific accountability appointment to do so. Setting it with us would be even better, because then we get to see you and help you directly.

## Deeper Forces at Play

Sometimes it's not enough to set a goal on paper and just go for it. We need to understand that we are hardwired in our body and brain to function the way that we do, and it might take more than positive thinking and checking boxes to get us across the finish line.

I am *right there* with a goal that I have right now. I've shared my ups and downs with weight over the years. I have lost everything except a

---

3    Thomas Oppong, "Psychological Secrets to Hack Your Way to Better Life Habits," *Observer*, March 20, 2017, https://observer.com/2017/03/psychological-secrets-hack-better-life-habits-psychology-productivity/

final 20 lbs. that I would like to trim off—but every time I do, my body works like hell to remind me that it is not safe to be so exposed—which is how I feel when I'm at my goal weight. I am certain that it stems from my history of sexual abuse and issues with setting appropriate boundaries. Regardless, it is so deeply wired inside of my body and brain that overcoming this next hurdle to my ideal health is going to take some very deliberate action, rewiring, and thoughtful reaction to overcome my beliefs and my body and brain's attempts to keep me right where I am.

As I write this, my next attempt begins … and it's about the 467th time since reaching my current health goals that I've set out to get to the next level, but I have to try. And I will continue trying until I get it. I must #KeepGoing.

And when I achieve that, I will celebrate. I will enjoy, and I will be grateful. I will have also reached the peak of that mountain, and from that vantage point will then see the other mountains I might scale. It might be another level of health, spiritual growth and development, or learning a new skill.

There will always be something new to learn and master. And I will always enjoy the journey of becoming the type of person who can achieve it.

People often ask me whether I would change anything about my life if I could. The answer is so easy for me, and it is that I would not. I really like who I am today. I like knowing that I can do anything— despite the odds. I like knowing that I have the skills, language, and talent to always be able to support myself, and knowing that whatever I lack, I can learn. I like knowing that I am a

> ◆
> I am grateful for every experience along my journey and the skills that I have now as a result.

resilient person. It makes me less afraid to try leveraging life's experiences, to try new things, to take risks, and to live completely and wholeheartedly.

I don't know that I'd like to follow a leader into battle who didn't have battle scars, so it makes sense that some of the greatest leaders are those who had to fight the hardest to get to where they are.

I am grateful for every experience along my journey and the skills that I have now as a result.

## Be the Bison and Face the Storm

Getting pregnant at fifteen and being faced with that decision taught me a *lot* of things, but most importantly it taught me the skill of facing things head-on and taking responsibility.

Bison are known to face storms and walk through them, knowing instinctively that it's the fastest route out. Facing things head-on is hard, but for me it's been the most efficient and healthiest way through.

## Take Responsibility/Ownership— Even When It's Not Your Fault

The sexual abuse that happened to me wasn't my fault. The results from that (me seeking inappropriate and unhealthy attention at an early age) also weren't my fault.

Going out with a twenty-one-year-old man who got a fifteen-year-old girl pregnant, that was 50 percent my fault. I'm sure the courts would argue otherwise … that it was 100 percent his fault, but at the end of all of it, I was 100 percent responsible for the outcome, regardless of what the courts or parents said.

In leadership and in business, this has come in *very* handy for me as a first response to challenges. I've never looked for whose fault it was; instead, I took ownership and decided how we would move ahead. Leaders take responsibility.

## "Tomorrow Isn't Guaranteed." No. Really. It's Not.

It's our experiences earlier in life that mostly shape our operating system as adults. When I was nineteen and my brother was twenty-three—he died. In an instant. Gone. Off the earth. No life. No possibility. No more beginnings, middles, or ends.

It is most likely a driving factor in my desire to live a truly full life. Understanding that tomorrow could very literally be my very last day on this planet. If it were, what would I be able to say about what I did while I was here? Is what I'm doing *right now* something I would be proud of doing?

That doesn't mean that I can't rest and relax. This isn't all about achievement; this is about *living*. Fully.

People say, "Tomorrow isn't guaranteed," but they say it with the lightness of a piece of driftwood with the saying "Live, Laugh, Love" painted on it at a beach house.

It's so much more than that. It's *life*. And it's not guaranteed. So *let's goooo*!!! Do something with it!

## Bloom Where You Are Planted

Many think that if they were in their dream job or opportunity, they would do better. Work harder. Produce better results. But what they don't realize is that the opportunity is here and now. The time to do our best work is right here and right now.

Long-term care and Medicare insurance didn't represent a sexy career path for me, but it was my best opportunity, and my partners, leadership team, and I maximized it in every way that we could.

I'm proud of that industry and the good that it does for our aging population, and I'm proud of the business we built within it. The opportunity isn't "over there." It's right here. Right now. Maximize it, and either the ideal opportunity will come along, or you will develop the skills necessary to figure out what's next.

# Recognizing When You're at a Crossroads

When I had to make a decision about my pregnancy, there was an obvious set of paths I had to choose from.

But it isn't always quite so obvious when we're faced with either this path or that one. It sometimes just gets buried in the busyness of life.

It might be that a person is overworked or in an unhealthy relationship or they might be physically unhealthy, but instead of distinctly seeing two paths (the one they are on vs. the one they could be on), they stay on the current path, because while it sucks, and a part of them is dying inside every day that they stay on it, the massive amount of energy required to make change is simply too much.

It's important that each person reading this book understands that we can choose a new path at any moment of our lives. We don't have to wait until we're at a breaking point. We don't have to wait until the first of the year. We don't have to wait for the milestone birthday or wait for someone else or some event to make the decision for us, like getting fired, a partner leaving the relationship, or a hospitalization. Waiting for external forces to decide for us is the opposite of taking responsibility and ownership.

It's why so many people don't make change. It is so much easier to continue in life as we are, because to demand something different means that we are 100 percent responsible for the outcome. It's *us* that made the decision to quit instead of the boss firing us. That's why it's so scary!

But here's the reason it's even scarier than you may have even known. Let's say that the issue we'd like to tackle is our poor health or strained wealth. It can be a tricky one to work on because the odds are that if we're really unhealthy in either category, so too are the other people we spend most of our time with.

What that means is that as soon as we start to experience some successes in changing our health or wealth status, we risk creating distance in our current relationships and, even worse, losing relationships entirely.

The reason *that* is so terrifying is because what we are really wired for as humans is love and connection and to be a part of a tribe. Our early-human brains need us to belong to a community because without our tribe, we would literally face death (if we were Neanderthals, of course … not today).

This is the dilemma of *not* being a Neanderthal but still having a Neanderthal brain. Our brain is telling us change = distancing from the tribe = death.

Not true anymore. While it can be painful, it doesn't mean death. We actually *can* survive if our relationship dynamics change. In this day and age, we are blessed with the option to keep our original tribe and also join new tribes.

These might be people who are deeply passionate about the things you are deeply passionate about. They share your same values, they are focused on the kinds of things you are focused on, they're supportive, and they are easy to be around.

Just because you were born into a particular family and fell into the friend circle you are in does not mean you share any of the above. It means that you carry some genes and DNA, or you happened to share some classes or work schedules, but your unique personality and life experiences may have formed your personality into one that is nothing like those currently around you. If you haven't yet made that distinction, it might be something worth a little exploration.

When I was in the process of making massive shifts and changes in my life in my twenties (which was the first time … but this happened again in my thirties), I changed or ended all of my friendships at the time. Most were not supportive of the vision I had for my life. I went solo for some time, just working on myself and my health and my career. It was lonely, there is no question, but I preferred to be alone vs. distracted. I felt like I didn't have time to waste, and this seemed like the most efficient path.

I'm not saying you have to go friendless; I'm saying be aware of the things that might be influencing your capacity to move forward.

# On Leadership

I was waiting for a long time to be told I was a leader. *Read that!* That doesn't even make sense. It's unfortunate I had to wait to take a test at a Tony Robbins event to learn I was a leader.

Leaders don't wait to be told; they just lead. They see an opportunity to step up, and they do it. They don't wait for permission.

Leaders also go first. I meet so many people who are in leadership positions who are afraid to go first, to be the first one to trust first, to be the first one to be vulnerable first.

It makes me think they should probably reconsider their leadership position or step up, because leaders go first. That's like … the definition of leading. And here's a fun fact: you won't get what you don't give in a leadership position. Or in any relationship, really … so give, and *ye shall receive*!

## Clarity Break

In EOS, we talk to leaders about the importance of clarity breaks. My first notable clarity break that I can recall was on my maternity leave with Liam. I'd been through so much in a very short time up until that break, having just lost my father-in-law, working to settle his estate, building our business, being pregnant, eye surgeries, etc. A break was long overdue.

One afternoon, I went for a walk. I had the space to think and just be. The connections I made in my head during that walk were that it was time to make a significant shift in our business and shut down my entire department and ultimately shift our product focus.

Clarity breaks mean *zero* work. *Zero* checking in. But when we take them, some of our very best work just naturally happens.

To get better results, we need to take breaks.

## Delegate and Elevate

This is a powerful EOS term and practice that I wish I'd learned much earlier in my career and life.

I always felt like I was less than because I couldn't figure out how to do it all. I never realized that the real question wasn't ever whether I could do it all to begin with. It was whether I *should*.

With everything that we do, there is an opportunity cost. If I choose to do this, then I can't do that. If I spend my time doing this $25/hr. task, then I'm missing out on the opportunity to do that

$100/hr. task. If I'm building the marketing campaign, then I'm not developing the next relationship.

What I realized over time is that the more I chose to do things that helped me increase my value and what I had to contribute, the better my life and my business got.

Gradually, I stopped doing things that I could delegate (at home it was housekeeping, at work it was marketing and operations) so that I could focus on things that helped me or us get farther faster.

## Steps to Take Now toward Your Very Best Life

When should you start working on all of this? I don't know … would *now* be a good time?

Since this is a system that will take time to put in place, I wanted to give you a couple of things you can do *right now* until you can get the good work of this system locked in.

**Step 1**: Go to maritautimes.com and sign up for emails and connect to our socials and community of peeps who are just like you and me.

**Step 2:** Schedule on your calendar right now to take your next steps. Consider one or all of the following three things to schedule:

1. Time with your partner to talk, dream, and share the tools, and/or

2. Time to go to maritautimes.com, print off the PDFs, and start following the program, and/or

3. Time on our calendar for a free coaching session to figure out what your next steps should be.

I can't wait to meet you and hear the stories of your amazing journey and how you've taken responsibility for your own life, growth and development.

To send you off with the exact perfect vibe, please look up "Try Everything" by Shakira from the Zootopia soundtrack. This is our theme song. Yours and mine. Turn it up and dance with me into our AMAZING FUTURES!!!